Life Is Something Else

Life Is Something Else

BY ELSIE GIBSON

A PILGRIM PRESS BOOK
from United Church Press, Philadelphia

Library of Congress Cataloging in Publication Data

Gibson, Elsie.
    Life is something else.

    "A Pilgrim Press book."
    Includes bibliographical references.
    1. Experience (Religion) 2. Gibson, Elsie.
3. Russell, Bertrand Russell, 3rd Earl, 1872-1970.
4. Beauvoir, Simone de, 1908-   5. Price, Eugenia.
6. Death. I. Title.
BR110.G48   218   74-13755
ISBN 0-8298-0286-X

The scripture quotations in this publication are (unless otherwise indicated)
from the *Revised Standard Version of the Bible*, copyrighted 1946 and 1952 by
the Division of Christian Education, National Council of Churches, and are
used by permission.

United Church Press, 1505 Race Street
Philadelphia, Pennsylvania 19102

CONTENTS

INTRODUCTION

MY MOTHER WAS DEAD.

A few days ago, numb with misery, I had gone into the orchard, picked up an apple, and set it in a fence corner. It was still there, no bruise visible. To a girl just turned fourteen, this said that her mother had been more perishable than an apple.

Now I was going to have to look at her in her casket. The thought suffocated me but adults insisted, saying I would be sorry if I did not see her this last time. Throat exploding, I went over to where she was and peered through the glass.

She was not there. Instantly I knew this, although no word of hope for life beyond death had been spoken. My mother would not be buried; she had gone.

Where? I did not know, but a penetrating peace wiped out the terror. Where did the peace come from? I could not have answered that either.

For a year we remained in the rural community to which we had come as strangers twelve months before. Our relation to the church had been marginal, but its members were kind, inviting us to dinner, and responding to our needs in other ways. Mrs. Bair, who had answered our call for help when my mother became ill in the night and who had stayed until relatives arrived, gave me a New Testament and encouraged me to pray. Faith was born or perhaps planted, like a seed, in my mind. Then we moved back to the city where faith, like everything else, was pulled in a dozen different directions. The plant started to die.

How could it have been otherwise? I could put the ring my father gave my mother in its little box, and it would remain intact. But how does one take care of faith and preserve it? Time, ongoing experience, and human relationships beat it down. That it flows on from generation to generation is astounding. It goes out of the world with every person who has ever believed and died. How does it traverse the chasm of these myriad deaths? How does it leap the generation gap, sometimes called the honesty gap? Or, what wind blows the fire through the centuries from one stand of perishable human beings to another?

Innumerable books have been written about faith from a theological point of view; this is not another of them. This is a show-and-tell book about the life to which faith leads, the life that is something else, but it is not autobiography in the usual sense. For here we shall be thinking about more than my personal experience. My method will be to look, also, through the eyes of three others who have revealed themselves extensively in their writings.

Experience is a tricky thing. It meshes elements of personal freedom, the sometimes very subtle influences of other individuals and groups, and the overall pressure of cultural surroundings in the most unpredictable ways. Have you ever noticed how an apparently trivial incident can spark phenomenal change in a person? An offhand remark may have repercussions out of all proportion to what was in the speaker's mind. No human being could ever untangle the mass of interrelationships through which we exalt or damn each other. We shall look into this more explicitly in the first chapter of Part I and see how it affected my three traveling companions, bearing in mind, naturally, that we are dealing with the impact of their self-revelations on me.

What if Bertrand Russell had met a Unitarian with the passion of a Martin Luther? What if the Roman Catholic priest had said something different to Simone de Beauvoir? What if Ellen Riley had not cared enough to venture a personal question to Eugenia Price? And what if Mrs. Bair had failed me in a second, more severe crisis years after my mother's death? Often the life that is meaningless and the life that is something else run as close together as the lanes of a superhighway.

Once the clergy would have had a neat solution to these questions: some are predestined to be saved and others to be lost. For many years the behavioral sciences have been saying much the same thing in other words: persons have been conditioned to become what they are. This point of view is challenged now, and even those who work with the mentally ill are saying that there is an area of freedom in everyone.[1] It may not be large, but there are options. What or whom to trust is a hard decision; usually we flounder for a time, but eventually we settle down upon some personal policy or belief.

Life is its testing ground—and then death. There are, of course, many little deaths in life: disappointments in people, the loss of someone we love, financial failure, disgrace, accidents leaving permanent disabilities, and countless other forms of suffering that put our ideas, whether religious or irreligious, on trial.

The final testing ground, nevertheless, lies beyond and is outside the ken of man. So all problems, social or personal, related to life's visible termination are fringed with mystery. Dogmatism, in the pluralistic milieu of the late twentieth century, convinces relatively few. I hope to show, though, that in the later decades of life a person is already breathing in the climate his experience has created and that this climate—not our fragmentary scientific knowledge—is the basis for the meaning or lack of it that we perceive in life and death.

Ultimately, there are only two world views: One affirms that man is alone on earth, and must make his way the best he can; the other declares that his pilgrimage is accompanied by Someone Else who offers clues to the life that is something else. In a world as distraught as this, one does not find meaning on the surface. Thus many are searching through the occult, through mysticism, through paranormal happenings for some inner validation of being. I have found that validity in Christian experience which, if it has any depth, must be regarded as a form of psychic as well as social experience. We shall try to clarify what Christian experience is in the second chapter of Part I.

Part II will be an examination of my own inner relationship to God, or, if one chooses, of my psychic experience with Christ and what came of it. I can readily agree with behavioral scientists that this is conditioned to a considerable extent by sociological environment, despite the fact that I grew up in a home that felt no need of the church. I am equally convinced, however, that there is an unconditioned space in which my freedom has been interacting with Another.

Death obviously comes, whatever the world view, and after death—mystery. Cope with it as we will socially (and I am devoting a chapter in Part III to that because Christians, like all others, are influenced by and help to influence the social order), what meets the eye is life culminating in death. Still, after fifty years of Christian experience, I am overwhelmed by the inward evidence that life is something else.

For nearly two thousand years Christians have witnessed to a life that is more than meets the eye. Why, when death is evidently the end, do they continue to do this? Are they afraid to face "reality"? Or have they found that reality is something else? How do you and I, or anyone else, know what reality is? And what if our wish to live or to die should, in the end, be granted? Would this make any difference now in the option we take up?

PART 1

Experience

CHAPTER 1

Experience: God and Death

As a young minister in Minneapolis, I was asked to speak at the YWCA one Easter morning and took as a text, "I give unto them everlasting life." Afterward a woman blurted out, "If what you say is true, it is the worst news I have ever heard. This life is enough. I don't want any more." In our nation alone, there are approximately 22,000 known suicides a year; suicide holds tenth place as a cause of death, second place among young people. Many persons (including some church members) who enjoy life have reconciled themselves to the idea that death is the permanent end. "This life is it; there isn't any more," a Protestant nurse told me. A Catholic nurse, questioned about her faith, said bluntly, "Faith is self-hypnosis."

Are such statements a brave acquiescence to scientific fact, or are they a deduction from experience? Can experience today lead to a different conclusion?

What Experience Is

In popular speech, experience is what has been lived through, but in a chapter on the subject such a definition is too vague to be helpful. For experience is lost if it is not thought about, and when we think about it, we must take into account the interaction of our minds with the events and relationships in which we participate. We will here note five points concerning experience.

1. First, normal minds are not empty. They have basic furnishings, meaning that they have patterns of thought picked up

from conversations overheard in childhood on politics, religion, and numberless subjects. Unconsciously we adopt attitudes of parents, teachers, friends, television favorites, books, etc. No bright child is going to believe all that he hears and, bright or not, we identify ourselves only with what we do believe. What we have accepted, then, become the *presuppositions* in the light of which we make up our minds about new happenings.

We cannot, however, go on to say that these presuppositions make an open mind impossible, or bind us irrevocably to the past. We can affirm that total objectivity is impossible and that persisting patterns of thought tend to identify us with recognizable groups of people. For instance, the man who is always spouting Marxist maxims should not be surprised if others dub him a communist, with or without his approval.

When science was younger, it used to be credited with complete objectivity as against religion, which was supposed to be subjective. But in the last decade or so, many scientists are themselves convinced that their work, too, is conditioned by presuppositions. The questions they ask and the experiments they design have a distinct relationship to theories they suspect may be true. Does not a theory place a presupposing tag of expectation upon an experiment: this is what we anticipate finding, else why the design? The theories on which evidence has been accumulating affect the formation of new theories. Sometimes scientists have to backtrack in the light of new and apparently contradictory discoveries, so they are constantly warning the press and public not to jump to premature conclusions. Any new theory, which through experimentation brings to light striking corroboration, opens wide vistas and sends the imagination skyrocketing. But scientists caution, reserve judgment, much more must be learned. "The history of science is full of stories of unlikely ideas which have eventually become accepted and apparently likely ideas which have come to grief," says John Habgood.[1] So, while scientists make every effort to be openminded and objective, they cannot climb out of their own skins in the interest of an experience freed from all presuppositions and interpretations, nor can anyone else.

As for presuppositions binding us to the past, one may insist that by forgetting them and keeping our eyes on the present and future, we can crawl out from under the crushing weight of ancestral mistakes. F. M. Esfandiary, whose dismissal of the past is wholesale, says, "The young modern is too pliant and dynamic to encapsulate himself within a distinct identity."[2] In his opinion, the writings of Plato and Confucius sound like a "boy scout manual"; biblical codes of morals suggest "regulations at a school of bad boys." But a label is placed on Esfandiary whether he wants it or not. He is a futurist, and he has his own presuppositions, the most questionable of which may well turn out to be that the past can teach us little or nothing.

All persons capable of learning feel they have already learned something. They confront the present moment with mental equipment in the shape of presuppositions.

2. A second factor underlying and conditioning experience, and always a part of it, is the focus of attention. Research on the human brain has not yet been able to produce a reason why we take an interest in one thing rather than another.[3] I sat in a favorite philosophy class one day, but my focus of attention was not where it belonged; it was on wedding plans, my future husband, and our coming honeymoon trip. The professor, sensing that I had been mentally absent for at least twenty minutes, suddenly tossed a query at me, "What do you think of that point, Miss Fuller?"

"I'm sorry. I didn't hear the last thing you said."

"What do you think of the next to the last thing then?" he asked with a twinkle in his eye. He was working for a refocus on philosophy, and it makes a great deal of difference in the long-range experience of a woman whether she gives her attention to academic subjects, a husband and family, or both. The prolonged focus of attention determines the tone of any life. It marks out the influences under which we place ourselves, the friends we choose, the areas in which we gather information, and finally becomes the raw material out of which our conception of what is believable, and what is not, emerges.

3. This does not mean change is impossible. It is a common

thing for people to shift their mental furniture around as time goes on. What is important to an individual at the age of fifteen may be pushed into a corner and all but forgotten by the time he is twenty. Friendships cool or heat up. We grow, find new ways of having a good time, possibly pass through pain or sorrow that causes us to rearrange our thinking. Change is normal. Experience is not static; it widens and sweeps along.

4. Moreover, change can, under the right circumstances, take place so rapidly and be so radical as to jolt a person out of all sense of his old identity. We will be noting this presently in the case of Eugenia Price. Where religion is concerned, this is called conversion, but it happens in other fields too. A teen-aged prisoner, depressed by what jail was going to do to his future, grasped the idea that people would revise their opinions of him if he could go to a different neighborhood, make new friends, and get a fresh start. Already labeled a "juvenile delinquent" by society, and facing the additional label of "criminal" because he was now legally a man, he found that he was still able to change fast enough to become a solid citizen. He did not let himself freeze into a predictable type. He did a right-about-face. So, change can be gradual or swift.

5. Experience cannot be separated from the language that expresses and further conditions it. It is impossible even to think without words. There is, of course, a nonverbal communication that may convey emotions words cannot express, but, as human beings, we are not limited to it. Complex thoughts and specialized purposes can be put into language and lead to levels of understanding and fellowship of a distinctively human kind. In making love, for example, what is felt may be cataclysmic, but what is said can give many shades of meaning to the experience.

In summary, then, what we live through, our experience, is affected to its roots by our presuppositions about life, by the way we focus our attention, by growth and interaction with other persons that bring smooth change, by the possibility of radical inner reorientation, altering the very goal and style of life, and by language.

With this in mind, we turn to the three persons whose autobiographies reveal a life history that I want to consider along with my own.

Bertrand Russell

Bertrand Russell, a "lovable agnostic" whose autobiography fills three sizable volumes, having lost both parents in early childhood, grew up in the home of his Anglican grandfather, Prime Minister of England, and his much younger Scotch Presbyterian grandmother. Alternately and impartially, he was taken to the two churches, but at home he was taught the doctrines of Unitarianism by his grandmother who became a Unitarian at the age of seventy. His childhood was reasonably happy but lonely, and his adolescence was plagued with problems related to faith in God. There was no one with whom he cared to discuss these problems, and eventually he came to the position that "Christianity of the existing kinds has had its day."[4] If the Unitarians had had a really great man like Luther, he thought, such a person might have been able to reinvigorate it, but no leader of that stature was in sight. Before entering Cambridge University, he was well on the road to agnosticism. Theodore Roszak quotes him as saying, "I would rather be mad with the truth than sane with lies."[5] As Roszak says, this would mean madness from the standpoint of others; one's own estimate of truth would be his standard of sanity.

A decisive mystical experience early in Russell's married life caused a permanent change in his personality. It happened at the home of Alfred North Whitehead, an intimate friend, when a heart attack threw Mrs. Whitehead into an agony of pain. Confronted by her suffering in the midst of his own self-centered happiness, he says, "The sense of the solitude of each human soul suddenly overwhelmed me." Within five minutes he saw that human loneliness is beyond endurance. Only "the highest intensity of the sort of love that religious teachers have preached" can penetrate it.[6] No other motivation works. In a flash of illumination, he felt close to everyone alive, saying that "one should penetrate to the core of loneliness in each person and speak to that." This experience was the root of his humanism.

Later, with a number of works on mathematics and philosophy to his credit, Russell, a pacifist and socialist, criticized both sides in World War I and was rewarded with a fine and prison sentence. Digging deeper he thought, "Human affection is at bottom an attempt to escape from the vain search for God." To love God, he believed, was to love a ghost and to become specter-like oneself. "Good people" disgusted him because of their mildness; they were "Sunday-schooly"; they did not know the volcanic side of human nature, lacked a sense of humor, had no intensity of will, "nothing of what makes men effective."[7]

That this was not an altogether harsh and arbitrary judgment is borne out by two of Russell's fellow-countrymen, both of whom are now ordained ministers. One says, "For me the Church had nothing to offer. It was grey and sad, attended by people who were not real, and led by persons who could not laugh, and who dressed as though they were part-time undertakers' assistants."[8] The other notes, "The impression still in my mind is of a rather dull and dismal atmosphere, tinged with the smell of incense."[9] Goodness lacked luster. Russell felt the desire that must have been satisfied in these men, to break out of the prison walls of his own nature; he was aware that cynicism and skepticism were imprisoning some great force for good within him. He sensed that this "ghost, from some extra-mundane region," was always trying to tell him something that he was to convey to the world, but he could not understand the message. "I feel as if one would only discover on one's death-bed what one ought to have lived for, and realize too late that one's life had been wasted."[10] Later, in the same vein, he wrote, "I feel I shall find the truth on my death-bed and be surrounded by people too stupid to understand —fussing about medicines instead of searching for wisdom."[11]

The need for clarity, the need to be in control of the facts, to be logical, to follow the scientific method, insulated him against belief in that which was too big for his mind to manipulate. He could not have faith without a clear map in his hands and was never able to accept the Christian teaching that God loved him, and asked his responding love, while he was trying to love his fellowman. But he was ambivalent. "Even when one feels nearest to other people, something in one seems obstinately to belong to God and to refuse to enter into any earthly communion—at least that is how I should express it if I thought there was a God."[12]

The love of wisdom did not replace the love of women in Russell's life. He married four times and had a number of mistresses. His rejection of the traditional Christian standard of morality will be viewed by some as sufficient reason why God was never more than a ghost to him. Are there not, after all, some divine commandments? Is it not a contradiction to be hankering for God on the one hand, and on the other to be making one's own rules with regard to the witness of two great world religions, Judaism and Christianity, on what constitutes acceptable conduct?

But Russell, far advanced in agnosticism, did not see it that way, and how can you hold a man who is neither Jew nor Christian to the moral codes of these religions? Does not full commitment to Christian standards of sexual morality follow faith rather than merit it?

On one occasion, however, Russell was not careful enough about his choice of words. Lecturing at Columbia University, he made the loaded statement that what the world needs is Christian love. An avalanche of letters descended upon him, believers rejoicing over his conversion, agnostics grieving his departure from their ranks. Russell was irritated:

I had thought it obvious that, when I spoke of *Christian* love, I put in the adjective "Christian" to distinguish it from sexual love. . . . If you feel this [Christian love], you have a motive for existence, a guide in action, a reason for courage, and an imperative necessity for intellectual honesty. If you feel this, you have all that anybody should need in the way of a religion.[13]

He had divorced the word Christian from Jesus and all churches following him with no sense of inconsistency and, one might add, without realizing his debt to the Christian tradition in his own early life. Christianity and humanism were one and the same thing.

Does a sensitivity to social problems that goes well beyond that of the average church member entitle one to view his actions as expressing "Christian love"? Is humanism Christianity at its best? Is a high degree of socialization the equivalent of Christian experience? Russell may have paid too little attention to the fact that noble birth and natural gifts had placed him with an intellectual elite and given him the ability to assess situations that the ordinary faithful, conditioned by inferior cultural advantages, could not share. The Christian church does not possess a magic wand that bestows vision and goodness overnight.

Bertrand Russell, who lived nearly a century, saw in his children a biological escape from death, but a "metaphysical" fear produced by the "cold universe" chilled him. He saw that whole universe as a prison. Long before his death he wrote, "There is darkness without, and when I die there will be darkness within. There is no splendour, no vastness anywhere; only triviality for a moment, and then nothing."[14] Subsequently, he was to express himself in another way that will be noted later, but he recoiled to the last from the cruelty in man and from man's ultimate powerlessness.

Simone de Beauvoir

We go now to France to observe a girl growing up in a Roman Catholic home under the guidance of a mother for whom religion was the very substance of life and a father who asserted full intellectual independence without leaving the church. A serious child, Simone de Beauvoir felt "penetrated by the presence of God." She believed that however little a person might keep from God, it would be too much if he existed, and however little one might give him, it would still be too much if he did not exist. She wanted to get closer to God but did not know how to go about it, and privately resolved, in early adolescence, to become a Carmelite nun—not an unusual phase, at the time, for devout Catholic girls. Such a high standard, though, kept her in a state of guilt, and she stopped receiving communion at Mass. In an effort to find herself, she borrowed the *Handbook of Ascetic and Mystical Theology* from a priest, and upon returning it went to confession, saying that she had not partaken of the sacrament for some time because she had lost her faith.

"What mortal sin have you committed?" the priest inquired.[15]

The encounter in the confessional was a failure, the priest considering her inability to mention a serious sin evasive in the light of her advanced reading. In her own eyes she became an outcast. Many years later she declared, "God had died when I was fourteen; nothing had replaced him."[16]

While the church had not helped her over the hurdle between early childhood religion and the tempests of adolescence, she did not relinquish longing for God entirely. "At certain moments, with all my defenses down, I would seek refuge in the side aisles of a church in order to be able to weep in peace; there I would prostrate myself with my head in my hands, suffocated by the bitter-smelling dark."[17] One night she "summoned God," asking that he show himself to her if he really existed. He did not come, so she stopped trying to speak to him. Just under twenty, she was torn between hunger for the holy and thirst for forbidden fun. Passionately in love with life, she could not decide whether its riches lay with God or with the world. That there might be some connection between love of God and love of the world's people seemed not to cross her mind.

Truth, however, drew her like a magnet and she decided that she would "consecrate the years to come to an unrelenting search" for it. Taking a degree in philosophy at the Sorbonne, she placed second to Jean-Paul Sartre, who became her intimate, life-long companion. She and Sartre sought truth together: "We made it our particular endeavor to go as far as it was humanly possible in the search for truth, to consider it from every aspect."[18] But, as an adult, she faced the continuing elusiveness of truth. There were times when she would burst into floods of tears which Sartre attributed to too much wine, but Simone herself suspected that intoxication, breaking down normal controls and defenses, prodded her toward unpalatable truth, forcing her to face reality.[19] Looking back from a later vantage point, she expressed the view that "life contains two main truths which we must face simultaneously, and between which there is no choice

—the joy of being, the horror of being no more."[20] It was doubly hard to face ultimate problems without God, but she faced them honestly.

Even as a child, the thought of her own death had so terrified Simone de Beauvoir that she "screamed and tore at the red carpet."[21] It seemed impossible to live her life with the horror of death approaching. "What do you do when you're thirty or forty and you think: 'It'll be tomorrow,' how on earth can you bear the thought?"[22] One does not get the impression that she was constantly obsessed with the fear of death, but rather that the dimension of depth in her life, coupled with the existentialist philosophy that views life itself from the standpoint of death's finality, brought recurring nightmares. She says it was as though "waking life were a too-rosy dream with death hidden in the misty distance, and in sleep I reach the truth, the heart of the matter."[23] Worried about a serious illness of Sartre, she says, "Our death is inside us, but not like the pit in the fruit, like the meaning of our life; inside us, but a stranger to us, an enemy, a thing of fear."[24]

Readers of the third volume of her autobiography, *Force of Circumstance*, wrote her that if she had not lost her faith, death would not terrify her so. She did not agree, and after the harrowing weeks preceding her mother's gruesome passing, she wrote, "There is no such thing as a natural death: nothing that happens to a man is ever natural, since his presence calls the world into question."[25]

Certainly anyone who looks beneath the surface of life turns up insoluble dilemmas, but the big issue between atheists and Christians is: what prompts the questions? Simone de Beauvoir sees man hurling his demands for answers into the vast void. Christian theologian Rudolf Bultmann sees the problem in reverse: God calls us, in our total personalities, into question.[26] This interior questioning may be evoked by God as an invitation to seek him.

Like Bertrand Russell, Simone de Beauvoir combines what Christians would call "moral laxity" with a high degree of intellectual integrity. She has been a compassionate person, suffering with the world's "have nots," and trying to understand social issues.

Atheistic existentialism is not a shallow philosophy. It can be, and has been, combined with a sense of responsibility and sympathy for the pain and grief of others. A number of French playwrights portray man as a victim of his natural and human environment. Like a rat in a labyrinth, he dashes about, not knowing which way to turn. At the same time, some atheists regard the responsible use of freedom as a top priority.[27] But, as a Christian, one must ask: To be responsible, by definition, is to be accountable, and if there is nothing beyond man, to whom is one responsible? If the answer is, "To humanity itself," this is an abstraction. How can one be responsible to a procession of the dying? From the atheistic point of view, the counterquestion can be raised: "Is not God, too, an abstraction?" I do not see how this question can be answered by those Christians who regard communication with God as illusory. The problem remains: What is the root of the questions that call for an answer— man or God?

Both Russell and de Beauvoir, top-flight intellectuals, had contact with religious leaders whose authority made their mediocrity the more unbearable, and they left the church. This does not guarantee that they went in the right or only possible direction. Suppose throngs were to follow them and others like them. Would devotion to humanity survive generations of agnosticism and atheism, or would a rank growth of selfishness squeeze it out? At this point we cannot know, for departure from an active faith in God has not had a sufficient hold on the culture for a sufficiently long time to show what it would produce. We must also ask how far these two brilliant persons were unconsciously influenced by the Christianity they encountered in shaping the value structures of their lives.

Has the erosion of religious faith been one of the factors spreading earthquake tremors through the ground of individual and social morality? Suppose it has. Could we agree that if religion is only a support to morality, without regard to the truth or falsity of its prime assumptions about God, then the sooner it goes the better? John Taylor, an atheist, would hold religion accountable for failure to progress more rapidly toward humanitarian goals, and speaks of a "religious illness" that he classes with mental illness and considers "blinkers" preventing the mutual cooperation of men.[28] But should it turn out that there is a correlation between widespread unbelief and low public morality (from the humanistic and not simply the Christian point of view), would this not have implications as to the nature of man and human society? Could it be that man's development, personally and socially, is related to what generations of believers have regarded as God's revelation of himself as author, savior, and guide of mankind, and could not the real tragedy lie in the fact that no way has been found of separating revelation from its accidental accretions so that it could be taken seriously by late twentieth-century man?

Eugenia Price

Now we are ready to take up a short autobiography written by an American woman when she was under forty.[29] Eugenia Price grew up in a pleasant, residential section of Charleston, West Virginia. The women of her family were energetically religious while the men neither denied nor affirmed their own faith. Eugenia, at an early age, sided with the men. Her mother and grandmother spoiled her. When she bit her baby brother's finger, they were sure she thought it was candy, and when she hit him over the head with a cologne bottle, she was just "experimenting." Jealousy was out of the question.

Eugenia thought of Jesus Christ as "someone with a black beard who was out to spoil my fun." Gossip overheard when she was taken to church struck her as unkind and added to her alienation from organized Christianity. After a course in comparative religion at college, she became an atheist, entering a church only once in the following eighteen years to attend her grandmother's funeral.

Genie Price learned to write for radio, did daytime serials and nighttime free-lance shows, then opened her own production office in Chicago. Her first tussle with death stemmed from the loss of a little English bulldog that she dearly loved. Lonely after the loss, she "felt death in me, too." Next, she struck a depression in her writing, ate until she became obese, and could think of no good reason for getting up in the morning. Fear, worry, and the suspicion that she was deceiving herself waged war on her ego. Going home for holidays, she avoided friends and vetoed her parents' suggestions for social affairs.

But Genie was haunted by a peculiar dream that occurred annually over a period of ten or twelve years. In it Ellen Riley, the friend who in early adolescence had taught her to smoke Old Golds and to hold her cigarette "like a woman," met her in an overgrown, tangled garden where children were laughing, not shrieking as they did in Chicago. Ellen would exclaim, "I'm glad to see you back again!" When the dream occurred, Genie said she felt "clean inside and not a bit tired" for several hours. (In the next chapter, where I shall be discussing paranormal experience in relation to Christian experience, I will return to this dream.)

On a diet and with a sagging spirit, Genie went home for a vacation. Surprisingly, her mother was able to talk her into phoning Ellen, whom she had not seen in years, and to her amazement she found herself inviting her old friend for a weekend visit, regretting instantly, upon an affirmative response, that she had saddled herself with a guest.

On the defensive when they met, for Ellen seemed to have changed little, Genie monopolized the conversation with accounts of her successful career in Chicago. "But you look so unhappy," Ellen said after awhile with her old-time frankness. "What's really the matter?" Daunted by the direct question that pushed the intervening years aside, reestablishing intimacy, Genie, on the verge of tears, gave vent to her real feelings. With no sense of superiority or self-importance, Ellen described her own Christian experience. She did not overdo it. They both enjoyed music, and presently Genie read some of her poems aloud, the poems that had "soul." Ellen said they reminded her of the language of the prophet Ezekiel in the Bible.

Genie laughed, but instead of burying the weekend at a bar,

she soon went to New York to see Ellen. By some strange chance, a friend gave her a copy of Thomas Merton's *The Seven Storey Mountain* to read on the way. As is well known, Thomas Merton was an atheist who became a Trappist monk, and the reading convinced Genie that "life does not end here."

Ellen was hostess of the dining room at Calvary House in New York City and had an apartment there. That would be too close to the church for comfort, so going to a hotel and having time on her hands till her friend finished work, Genie spied a Gideon Bible that brought to mind the comparison between her poems and Ezekiel. She began to read, and under a spell that was little short of hypnotic went on and on, reading from many parts of the Bible while the hours sped by.

Her response to the penetrating truth and beauty of what she read was a broken prayer, "O God . . . O God . . . O God . . . O God . . ." Radical personality change in adult life can be a frightening experience, and Genie was afraid she was losing her mind. When Ellen came, she told her she wanted to die. Ellen's cheerful reply was, "It would be a good thing if the *old* Genie Price would die."

"O.K. I guess you're right," was Genie's forthright answer— and her own experience as a Christian began. Knowing her friend's uncompromising nature and how fragile her new life would be if isolated, Ellen went to Chicago to give moral support. A hard look at her job had made Genie decide she would have to choose between the work she had been doing and something more constructive. How could she go on writing murder stories for children to watch and trying to talk adults into doing what she would no longer do herself? The two faced rough going for a while and Genie's ego took a severe beating, but the result was that she became able to develop a new life-style. She found an opportunity for creative Christian broadcasting, and turned out to be a prolific writer whose simple, direct books for lay persons have sold into the millions of copies.

The death of her father forced Genie to face the uncertainty of life, and she found comfort in a sentence from an old book by Dwight L. Moody, "The essential self of our loved ones does not ever lose consciousness."[30] She was "gloriously aware" of its credibility as she looked at her father in his coffin and "saw only a bad photograph of his real living self."[31]

Cultural Experience

We have examined five facets of individual experience and considered briefly the response of three persons to the Christian environment into which they were born, noting especially their thoughts about God and death. Growing up respectively in England, France, and the United States, they reacted negatively to three types of institutional Christianity. Their individual experiences were different, but could their rejection of the church have been based upon common cultural experience?

If we probe this question, it becomes evident that Bertrand Russell, Simone de Beauvoir, and Eugenia Price had no thought of rejecting truth when they left the church. Breathing in the atmosphere of relativism that pervades our culture, they felt they were taking an honest, realistic step. At the age of eleven, Bertrand Russell had had his first glimpse of how uncertain the certainties were. Someone had told him that geometry "proved things," so he was enthusiastic when his eighteen-year-old brother offered to teach it to him. It was still "Euclid," and his brother began with the definitions; these were easy to accept, but when he was told about the axioms he would have to *assume,* he was indignant. What good is it to "prove" something if you have to begin with an unproved base? His brother said if he would not accept the axioms they could not go on,[32] but there was now a question mark over the validity of mathematics and everything else.

Simone de Beauvoir came to the same doubts by a different route. She had been taught the way to refute objections against "revealed truths," but knew no way to establish those truths themselves. They had to be taken for granted on the authority of the church which was never established to her satisfaction. So freedom and skepticism seemed a more sincere stance to these two intellectuals and others like them, than standing firmly on shaky ground.

When one rejects all religious belief, though, it is upon still other assumptions that are invisible because they are intrinsic to the present culture. We must assume that each individual is capable of digging out a truth to live by on his own. Truth becomes an inside matter, wholly subjective, and it is not surprising that moral standards, upon which there has been sufficient agreement to make legislation possible in the past, go by the board.

This utter relativism rests back upon another assumption: that there has been no accumulation of truth through the centuries, that the past has had nothing of solid, objective value to pass on to the present, that the search starts here. These assumptions, hard as it may be to put a finger upon them because of their general acceptance, should be seen for what they are—assumptions. But suppose mankind has found, or received, substantial truth in the past, suppose the individual is incapable of discovering a working truth in an isolated search. Is it not at least conceivable that our culture is now suffering from deprivation of truth in the midst of the tremendous explosion of knowledge? Can we be certain that our late twentieth-century view of the human situation is definitive?

Let us go back a way to see how we arrived at such popular assumptions. For centuries science had to struggle against the stranglehold of religious authority. Bit by bit, it broke free, demolished superstitions, and shattered ecclesiastical exclusivism where judgments of truth were concerned. Slowly public respect for its method grew. Wasn't it giving men a good life so that they could straighten their shoulders and enjoy leisure? Wasn't it freeing women from drudgery and making it possible for them to enjoy social activity and work on community projects? Young persons thrilled to the new fields opening up opportunities for advancement and a higher standard of living. Then came the world wars, the invention and production of more and more devastating forms of destruction, and the present ecological quandary.

Cultural experience does not parallel individual experience. When cultural change is taking place gradually, it is so slow as to be imperceptible because all of us are involved, and there is no one on the outside to call attention to it. But it gains momentum, and by the time astute members of society realize where we are heading, it is difficult to put on the brakes, bring events under control, and avoid gigantic threats to human survival.

Some years ago I prepared a course of study for parents on contemporary Christian personalities. Husband-wife teams who could serve as models of Christian life and service were proposed to me by various church leaders, and I corresponded with them. In family after family, I was struck by the fact that the college-age young people were preparing for careers in the physical sciences. From these outstandingly Christian homes, very few were selecting courses in the humanities or in religion. My study, had I been able to evaluate it properly at the time, was a sample, revealing that the switch from the influence of religion to the influence of science was rapidly gaining momentum.

The situation has become sinister, not through any fault of science itself, but because of our cultural enmeshment with it which shows up in several ways. First, the average person is not adept at sorting out theories from established facts. When an exciting discovery is made in research on animal brains, for example, newsmen immediately converge upon the scientist, as though he were a prophet, wanting to know what his research augurs for man himself and where it may lead. Even though faithfully reported, his words of caution as to what his work demonstrates are in vain. Small fact and burgeoning public imagination intertwine, and science fiction is soon busily spinning out apocalyptic visions that make those in the Bible appear trifling by comparison.

A second development has been that science is popularly regarded as monolithic, uniform in all its findings. The fact is, as Jacques Barzun pointed out some time ago, that, by the middle of the twentieth century, there were already fifty thousand scientific journals, publishing some two million articles a year—forty thousand a week. Even the abstracts produced by two hundred organizations filled volumes, many of which were the size of an unabridged dictionary.[33] Such voluminous findings cannot be kept correlated, nor do they necessarily corroborate each other. Individual scientists do well to keep up in their own special fields.

So scientific advance on many fronts makes it impossible to give even an approximate picture of what "science teaches." Yet a popular scientism has evolved that gives to its idol an authority fully as absolute as the church was ever foolish enough to claim in its proudest hours—and with no more justification.

This, I believe, has brought about an eclipse of religious truth that has plunged us into moral and spiritual darkness, illustrated by the demand that religion be secular (bound by this time) and relevant to the scientific-technological mentality. More insidious, however, is the popular deduction, among many clergy and laity alike, that "it is no longer possible to believe" some of the basic affirmations of the Christian faith. On precisely what grounds it is no longer possible to believe is not made clear. For such a statement to have scientific weight, all the facts would have to be in. And we are still a long way from the totality or unity of truth, assuming there is such a thing, which, at this point, can neither be affirmed nor denied with scientific certainty. Either way it is an affirmation of faith.

As an illustration relevant to the purpose of this writing, let us consider the status of the question of human consciousness after death. Many devotees of scientism are ready to say that consciousness comes to an end when people die, but as a matter of scientific fact, this is far from settled. Adequate theories even regarding the higher mental processes have yet to be formed. There are at present five possibilities relative to the brain and consciousness: (1) consciousness and brain mechanism cannot be distinguished; (2) they are closely linked; (3) they are loosely linked; (4) they are separate but coexistent; (5) they are separate.[34] The last possibility conceives of consciousness as capable of existing outside the body, or after death. Brain research has uncovered nothing up to the present time to make belief in the divine origin of the human mind impossible from a scientific point of view.[35] Freud, in contrast to some American psychiatrists, did not identify mind and brain,[36] and Jung stated that the psyche's attachment to the brain could be affirmed with far less certitude in his day than fifty years previous to that.[37] I wish to argue nothing from the above, save that we face an open question.

Or, to take another illustration, the development of computers that can think, feel, and will is seen as a further threat to faith in a transworldly destiny for man. But here again it is necessary to distinguish carefully between what has already been achieved and what is being forecast. Forecasts have a way of attracting the spotlight and disappearing into oblivion without notice.[38] In this connection, Nigel Calder remarks, "If a psychical theory of the twenty-second century should prove consciousness to be an inevitable consequence of certain laws of complex systems, you would still have to explain why these laws existed."[39]

There is no necessary cleavage between scientific and religious knowledge.[40] In swinging from religious authoritarianism to the authoritarianism of scientism, there has been a continual oversimplification of methods for reaching knowledge. Does not what we want to learn have something to do with the means we employ? Does it seem reasonable to approach a microbe and God in the same fashion?

There are two further factors in our cultural experience (as related to the purpose of this book) that may simply be mentioned as they have been explored at length by many writers. One is the prevalence of materialism. Young persons have suggested that the honesty gap is more difficult to bridge than the generation gap. They see our culture as one that gives lip service to Christianity and life commitment to material values. Eugenia Price felt the drive among her elders to "make good," to "get ahead." The church does not make a practice of contrasting such goals with the call to Christian discipleship, but the ambiguity exists between material and spiritual goals in the adult world, evoking the cynicism of youth.

Our cultural experience, further, includes violence and death on a massive scale, partly because of increased population and more sophisticated means of destruction, but also because the mass media keep us aware of evil all over the world. So, in summary, the relativity of truth, scientism, materialism, violence, and death permeate the intellectual atmosphere in which our minds breathe.

Christians do not escape it; they do not exist in a vacuum. Insofar as they live their faith, they affect the culture through their shared thought and action, but they are also conditioned, to a lesser or greater extent, by their culture. Some groups of Christians develop countercultures or subcultures of their own.

But what does it mean to "live your faith"? A year or so ago, sociologist Peter Berger addressed a group of ministers. In concluding his remarks he said, "Trust your experience." He paused and then with emphasis, added, "Trust your *Christian* experience."

"What *is* Christian experience?" one of the men asked. It was a rhetorical question and no discussion followed. This is the subject we shall consider in the next chapter.

CHAPTER 2

Experience: Christian, Mystical, and Paranormal

THE WORD CHRISTIAN IS VERY OLD AND USED TO HAVE A PRECISE meaning. It was coined in Antioch of Syria, the modern Antakya, Turkey, quite possibly by the police or public officials, to designate those who followed Christ and sang hymns to him. From a political point of view, any group pledged to a leader would bear watching. But, over the centuries, the term has proved elastic, and today, it is so vague as to be almost meaningless. It is applied, as we have seen in the case of Bertrand Russell, to those who accept a purely humanistic version of the teachings of Jesus without reference to him personally or to any of the churches that bear his name. Colloquially, it has a still wider sense, and may refer to any decent, respectable person. So, as might be expected, "Christian experience" has many shades of meaning, and one must be familiar with the language habits of the user before he can be certain of what the phrase implies in conversation or public address. This may be why many avoid its use now and profess ignorance of its significance. Probably most people would still agree, however, that Christian experience is something that is supposed to be taking place within the churches, so let us begin there in considering its meaning.

Types of Christian Church Experience

Churches fall into three broad groups, each encompassing a wide variety of viewpoints: 1. Conservative and pentecostal churches urge hearers toward conversion, involving radical change in adults, young persons, and sometimes even children. These churches stress a conscious relationship with God, Bible study, prayer, and witness that, put into practice, will re-form an individual's very identity. 2. Liberal churches, too, promote change, but in a less upsetting way. They encourage the hearer to adopt new motifs for action with the expectation that his earlier preoccupations will drop away or be pushed to one side. He is asked to invest time, money, and energy toward such ends as racial justice and peace. A different focus of attention will then bring smooth change. 3. Still other churches accent the sacraments as the structure par excellence through which God acts upon man, eliciting his response. One enters the Christian life through baptism. He confesses his sins, either to a priest or in the congregation, and receives assurance of pardon. He discovers his vocation, joins frequently in the eucharistic meal, and, finally, is made ready for death.

These three styles of church life are not mutually exclusive and cannot be sharply differentiated. Conversion occurs in all churches; nearly all have some commitment to social action. Few fail to regard at least two sacraments (baptism and the Lord's Supper) as a high and holy part of their life. It is a question of emphasis, but that emphasis does have certain repercussions. Let us look at a few of them, the negative ones first.

In conservative churches, especially those that, from time to time, call evangelists, the interior standard for converted persons may be fixed so high that one aims at it and fails over and over again. Concluding that he has not really been converted at all, a sensitive individual may go in and out at the gate of the Christian life, bogged down by guilt. Many reached by Billy Graham's campaigns are church members who, under the stimulus of his preaching, question whether they have ever been genuine Christians or not, and make a fresh, and sometimes more effective, start in their religious lives. But others less sensitive, instead of calling themselves into question, feel that an initial conversion, to which they can look back, gives them a through ticket to heaven—their sins are covered. As Gandhi once tersely observed, "Obviously, they are." Still others, on an even keel, keep self-examination private and, with the help of God, progress toward maturity.

Liberal churches, while helping themselves plentifully to ministers brought up in fundamentalist circles, complain that conservatives pay little attention to the need for social change. But liberals, too, face problems. Except for those who come up through their own church schools, they receive relatively fewer adults on confession of faith. Their approach, as I have said, is that of gradual conversion, and there is the constant danger that persons with a pagan outlook will be warmly welcomed into church membership while remaining blissfully unaware of what it should mean. The questions put to them at the beginning were open to varied levels of interpretation; baptized in infancy, they may have been received without the requirement of confirmation classes or the equivalent and, as a result, they enter the church with the idea that there is no real content to the gospel. Stress upon democracy leads to the subconscious (or even conscious) view that the church's message and mission have no sanction other than the majority vote of its members. National leaders of such churches repeatedly berate the laity for failure to obey a gospel that was not originally presented to them as calling for considerable change in thought and action. Too much was taken for granted by the church as well as by its incoming adult members.

Turning now to churches that center on the sacraments, we find problems of another kind. Sacramental religion may foster a high type of Christian mystical experience. On the other hand, the form of the sacraments may stand in the way of their end or purpose. It is possible for outward ritual to camouflage inward hollowness. Quiet worship in beautiful churches, with familiar words and heavenly music, may furnish a backdrop for escapism, and the emptiness may not be uncovered until tragedy strikes. Novelist Storm Jameson portrays a church member in the depths of misery, trying to get help from a clergyman who, seemingly unable to rise above platitudes, encourages him to pray.

"To whom shall I pray?"

"O come now," the uneasy priest protests, "you are not a child. You know . . ."

"I said, 'To whom shall I pray?' " The pseudo-religion of culture and intellectual elitism could not furnish an answer.

Positive Christian experience, of course, goes on in all churches. The broad difficulties indicated do not necessarily apply to individuals, congregations, or denominations.

The Essence of Christian Experience

With the growing impression that the churches' common experience transcends their serious differences, the twentieth century has seen many movements toward unity as well as a polarization of opinion regarding it. Those favoring church union see two tragic effects of continued divisions. By their failure to act for the healing of long-standing ruptures, Christians affirm that: 1. They love their own denominations more than a church clearly visible to the world. Unity in diversity and diversity in unity are not identical; the *encircling* fact stands out. 2. In an effort to make separation plausible, they focus on points on which it is impossible to see eye to eye while obscuring, by default, the bond that could, if fully grasped and lived, lead to an inner unity so great that outward divisions would be tolerable no longer.

Others just as sincerely feel that the effort to accent that common bond would impoverish everyone. Rich heritages would be washed away. Doctrinal indifferentism would result. Moreover, the practical difficulties of uniting structures and methods, congealed after generations of development, would divert attention from other important programs and demand financial investments out of all proportion to the gains of merger, especially in view of the growing spirit of cooperation and respect for differences among church bodies.

Young persons, seldom adequately represented at policy-making levels, are so impatient with denominationalism that many would gladly dispense with structures altogether and join in a spontaneous movement of unstructured Christian discipleship; they may not realize that group experience always tends toward the organizing process. That the entire Christian church is passing through an extremely trying period in which no confident prediction can be made about its future polity needs no further comment. Structures are important for many reasons, but the Consultation on Church Union[1] has discovered that structure is also the chief stumbling block to union. Resolving the problem will require wisdom and willingness to experiment.

The fact remains that Jesus, when asked to give his teaching in a nutshell, responded, according to the Gospels, with a concise directive: You must love the Lord your God with all your mind, will, emotion, vitality, and strength, and you must love your neighbor as yourself.[2] The first part of this response, love God, posed no problem to the understanding of his audience. Jewish men and women in the first century had listened to this instruction thousands of times—at home, on pilgrimage, going to bed, getting up. It was the one thing drilled into them: "Hear, O Israel: The Lord our God is one Lord; and you shall love the Lord your God with all your heart, and with all your soul, and with all your might (Deut. 6:4-6)." Having no image on which to concentrate, they still knew that their fathers had one deity on whom the people depended. They had entered into covenant with him; he had given them sworn promises and the holy law which, when obeyed, would insure this ongoing relationship. Their greatest leaders had interpreted their national history in these terms. So Jesus' words were not new to them.

The second part of his reply, love your neighbor, though, did perplex them, for they were sure he meant more than being kind to the family next door, whether friend or stranger. "Who is my neighbor?" a lawyer publicly inquired.[3] Jesus' answering tale of the good Samaritan has sunk into the very core of the cultural heritage of Western civilization. Anyone who has had minimal Christian education knows the story. When it was dramatized in Sunday school, all of us (little devils that we were) wanted to be the robbers. The good Samaritan had to be drafted and the victim, not by choice, was invariably a girl. But we got the message all the same: A person whose need confronts us is our neighbor, and our adult consciences, in or out of the church, squirm uneasily when we refuse to help.

We know the neighbor, but today we are not at all sure we know what is meant by God. Who is he? Further, how can one be commanded to love? If love of God is to be more than fantasy, must we not have some knowledge of him to evoke it? How can love that, by definition, implies relation be beamed into a void toward an unseen, unknown one? For a long time, it has seemed simpler to avoid the whole question by saying that the call to love God and neighbor coalesces into the one call to love the neighbor. Does not the Bible teach that whatever we do for others is accepted by Christ as done for himself?

True as the affirmative answer is, Jesus did not roll God and neighbor into one package like this, and man continues to crave a knowledge of whoever or whatever is responsible for his being here. An anthropologist, asked why he endangered his life by digging for hours in the hot sun, replied, "I want to find out who I am." So we dig. While the neighbor, according to Jesus, is authorized to receive our gifts of love to God, he cannot go proxy for God in kindling that love—not if he is unattractive. And if he is appealing, no command is needed.

The second directive flows from the first as well as making it concrete and visible on earth. But when we try to speak of Christian experience in other than humanistic terms, we face the dilemma as to what it is and how we find our way into it. Asking the churches that are supposed to have the answer, we are met by the three possibilities on which we have already commented: be converted, cast your lot with the "people of God," and learn by degrees what it means to live in that fellowship, express your desire to God and the church, and be baptized, learning through the mystery of the sacraments, appointed by him, to receive and give his love.

No doubt each answer is true in theory. But how does the theory clothe itself with flesh and blood? This is the question I want to try to answer, from a personal point of view, in Part II. I do not intend to offer myself as a model, but as one illustration of what can happen to the person who takes seriously the call to love God and neighbor.

As soon as Christian experience is differentiated from ordinary human experience, it prompts questions: "Is it mystical? What if one does not have a mystical temperament?" "A relationship with *God*? That sounds as though it would have to be occult, or at least beyond the normal." Since the mystical and paranormal have to do with the psyche and are not always clearly distinguishable from Christian experience, it seems important to take time to consider them separately.

Mystical Experience

Mysticism has been defined as the art of union with reality or the science of love,[4] but both "reality" and "love" have worn so thin that the definition no longer denotes anything specific. What would a union with reality be like? Today there are as many definitions of mysticism as there are differing conceptions of reality. Reality has been described as one of those "red-hot words" with a "cosmic glow" that ought to be avoided in speaking and writing because of its fuzziness.[5] Nevertheless, since mysticism, to the person involved, always seems at least quasi-religious in character, and with the wide connotation of "Christian" may seem Christian in character as well, let us pursue the point.

We may note, then, several kinds of mysticism.

1. Anyone who can find a beautiful outdoor spot on a rare June or bright October day must know what natural mysticism is. A man is part of nature and, lying on the grass, looking at the sky, he feels his oneness with all that is most real. Naturalist W. H. Hudson put the feeling this way:

The blue sky, the brown soil beneath, the grass, the trees, the animals, the wind, and rain, and sun, and stars are never strange to me; for I am in and of and am one with them; and my flesh and the soil are one, and the heat in my blood and in the sunshine are one, and the winds and tempests and my passions are one. I feel the "strangeness" only with regard to my fellow-men, especially in towns. . . . They are not of my world— the real world.[6]

In this mood, Hudson saw city man's works, sports, pleasure, even ideals as false, spawned by artificial life, "little funguses cultivated in heated cellars."

Going home after a day in the open, one often feels refreshed. The experience is not inherently Christian although it may combine with Christian experience, as in the case of Francis of Assisi, or be mistaken for it. W. H. Hudson himself, baptized in an English Methodist Church in Buenos Aires, attended public worship frequently, but found natural mysticism more intelligible than "button-holing the deity." His mother was a Quaker.

2. A second kind of mysticism centers in union with other human beings and may take two quite different directions: sexual mysticism, as in Henry Miller's writings, or humanism, as with Bertrand Russell.

The mysticism that finds cosmic significance in sex is unrelated to the purpose of this book, and I shall not dwell on it. It has been well explored by Arthur Gibson in chapter three of his book *The Faith of the Atheist,* where he treats the works of Henry Miller.[7] When a man and woman have consummated their union by the sexual act in a manner that involves the total personality of each, they have had one of the high experiences of earth, a true "peak"—transcending individual solitude and rising to a potential sharing in the creative joy of God. But men and women often try for such fulfillment again and again, and fall short of it, thinking the partner may be to blame: he or she does not love enough, respond sufficiently, give enough, and what promised to be ecstasy leaves a dull distaste. This may be true within or outside marriage. Even when union has been satisfying, no human being can perfectly live up to what it implies and promises. Quasi-religious and mystical as the experience may have seemed, it cannot deliver ultimate satisfaction. No man or woman can replace God. But there are many who never stop searching for the perfect complement to themselves.

3. A measure of this frustrated hope was doubtless present in Bertrand Russell, but we are concerned here with the humanism that stemmed from his dawning mystical awareness at the time of

Mrs. Whitehead's illness and that he called "Christian love" to distinguish it from sexual love. He believed the humanism he felt was all that anyone needed in the way of a religion, despite the fact that a "ghostly" God pursued him for some time.

Russell's position was not without some apparent biblical support. The apostle Paul had said, "All the law is fulfilled in one word, even in this; Thou shalt love thy neighbour as thyself (Gal. 5:14, KJV)." The First Letter of John states, "He that loveth not his brother whom he has seen, how can he love God whom he hath not seen (1 John 4:20, KJV)?" But there are two reasons why we cannot quite equate these sayings with humanism. First, all New Testament writings exhibit full awareness of the primacy of love for God as the root from which true love of neighbor springs. The Jewish community and early Christian communities were steeped in this knowledge. If love of the neighbor was not manifested, however, it could be assumed that any alleged love of God was spurious. A second point to notice is that the neighbor and the brother are never merged into an abstraction like "humanity" or "mankind." A specific person toward whom we have particular responsibility is taken for granted, not a nebulous "everybody" for whom it would be impossible to take up universal obligation.

Because Bertrand Russell was trustful enough to open his life to the world, an illustration from his *Autobiography* will clarify one distinction between humanism and Christian love. It has to do with the delicate and difficult question of his first divorce, on which we shall reflect without any thought of passing judgment. The marriage had not followed quickly upon "love at first sight," but had been a mutual commitment of two mature persons. In fact, it had not been easy for Bertrand Russell to win his first wife. He terminated the marriage when he found that he no longer loved Alys and the divorce was without bitterness. But at the age of eighty-one, she sent him the brief paragraph regarding their marriage that she proposed including in her *Memoirs*, offering to shorten it if it did not meet with his approval. Russell included it in his own *Autobiography*. It concludes, "Unfortunately, I was neither wise enough nor courageous enough to prevent this one disaster from shattering my capacity for happiness and my zest for life."[8]

Divorce is so painful that young persons today wonder, as Jesus' own disciples did, if marriage itself is worth the chance, if changeable human beings should ever enter into such a permanent agreement. A sexual relationship within marriage, but without love, seems more immoral to many than such a relationship outside marriage but with love. What does a person do, then, if marriage is to be kept inviolate, and the love of one partner has died? Suppose one wishes to follow Jesus' directive, "You shall love your neighbor as yourself," but love for husband or wife has simply ceased to exist, while the other partner still loves and wants to stay married? Does one love himself and leave with as much kindness and generosity as possible, as Russell did, or does he love his partner better and stay, inflicting the pain upon himself? In an impasse like this, what does Christian love ask? Humanism does not narrow the problem to this extent.

It seems quite clear, from the New Testament record, that Jesus did not intend to legislate on the issue, but rather to express the divine intention to enlighten man, not to enslave him. Since loving one's neighbor and loving oneself are, in the above instance, contradictory, and both self-love and love of the other are enjoined, is there any way out of the dilemma? It seems to me that the only recourse is to the first commandment and an effort to discover in prayer how the primary obligation of life— to love God—can best be fulfilled. Much will depend upon the maturity of the person who prays.

Many religionists will be inclined to say that self-sacrifice, as exemplified by the cross of Jesus, is the solution. This is not obvious to me, for I do not believe that Jesus faced death because he loved man. What love of man involved was ambiguous. Could he not have argued within himself that his life would serve men and women better than his death? I believe Jesus followed the implications of his love for God, praying in the Garden of Gethsemane for deliverance from death, but not at any price, waiting for the divine word that, strangely enough, Judas brought when he came with the soldiers. It was not a wholly new word but the word, heard in crisis, that confirmed all the others.

The love of man is not enough for the crucial decisions of life from the Christian standpoint; it is the love of God that must reveal in each individual case where true love of man lies. Self-sacrifice for other human beings, *as a principle*, is masochistic. It may actually harm them at times. The Christian sacrifices himself to God who then gives him to the world in such a way that the divine stake in any situation is saved. Jesus did not throw himself away for man. On several occasions, he slipped out of potentially violent situations, but when his "hour" came, he was ready to act with and for his Father.

There is a second point to be made with regard to humanism and Christian love, but before discussing it, it may be well to look at the word humanism more closely. It is one of the slippery terms with which differing ideologies have an incessant tug of war. Erich Fromm, for example, defines it as "the belief in the unity of the human race and man's potential to perfect himself by his own efforts."[9] Christians accept the first part of this definition but have reservations about the second: is this perfecting done without God?

The point is not minor; it differentiates those religions that have a belief in one holy God from all forms of altruistic agnosticism and atheism. To take the phrase Christian love and apply it to agnostic humanism not only leaves out its most important ingredient, love of God, but presents the average man with a task beyond his powers—"to perfect himself by his own efforts." A common error of the intellectual and social elite is the illusion that they are self-made. But they are not, for either money for education has been available to them, or, if not, they have been motivated from childhood to a recognition of its crucial importance. Often they have been exposed for years to the broadening effect of travel and casual conversations of leaders from many walks of life; they have been through a privileged socialization process that is inaccessible to the majority. If, in addition to this, they have grown up under the influence of parents or other relatives and close friends with deep religious commitment and a philanthropic spirit, they may go far, far beyond most Christians in their service to other human beings, and they deserve praise for making good use of their advantages.

But Christian love is a misnomer for what they are doing unless they are acting out of the prime motive of love for God. There is in Christian love a recognition that human beings can be so conditioned through childhood and youth that they literally cannot respond effectively to human love, much less initiate a relationship of love, without divine help. So, while humanism, apart from the love of God, can and does produce some of the most gracious and generous individuals in the world, it is not good news to the person who needs more help than man can give to make something of himself. For this reason, I believe that humanism, even when it springs from a sense of mystical oneness with mankind, can never be regarded as the equivalent of Christian experience.

4. Mysticism, as we have seen, may be unrelated to Christian experience, or it may be a narrower term, only partly covering it. When it comes to the mysticism of other religions, their relationship to Christianity is problematic. Institutes for the Study of Religion are cutting a path through the maze of ignorance that, for centuries, divided Eastern and Western quests for the meaning of life.

Religious experience, to be compared, must be known from the inside as well as through its sociological manifestations, but few have intimately known the inside of more than one of the world's great religions. Whenever conversion occurs, there is always the possibility that the convert has left the lower level of one faith to respond to the highest in another. When persons look to the East in search of the truth which the Christian faith has not made real to them, the depth of their exposure to it is always open to question. We must be fair enough to add that the reverse may also be true. Missionaries have noted that conversions to Christianity among those of primitive religions are numerous, among those of advanced religions few.

A humbler attitude is now developing among Christians, not because we have any less confidence in our own Lord, but because we have become aware of how unacquainted we are with the resources of other people. Frank Laubach learned this when he tried to work among the Moros of Mindanao. Efforts at conversion were futile, but lovers of the Qur'an were willing to sit down with him and, in a spirit of mutual respect and love, engage in study.[10] A similar attitude has taken Benedictine monk Aelred Graham to Asia where he has been able to talk with genuinely holy men without the least suspicion of patronage.[11] Such contacts are difficult, and preparation must be made for them, but they are not impossible, and they should be fruitful in enabling us to see what Christian and other types of religious mysticism have in common and where they differ.

The path to better understanding, however, lies even nearer because representatives of the religions of India, for example, are coming here. Maharishi Mahesh Yogi insists that he is teaching a technique rather than a religion in Transcendental Meditation, but this technique springs from an ideology that testifies to other Lords and other scriptures.[12] Whether this will lead to the convergence of world religions or to coexistence with mutual caring and trust cannot be foreseen.

Christian Mysticism Versus Activism

We have distinguished four kinds of mysticism (natural, sexual, humanistic, and Eastern), and discussed them in relation to Christian experience, noting an overlap in places. No one would question that Francis of Assisi was a nature mystic as well as a Christian. The church's program of social action may be confused with humanism in general, but it is motivated by love of God as well as man, though it may not articulate its theology in a manner satisfactory to all Christians. Christianity, while growing fast in the West, began in the East, and has always had its Eastern churches with their own mystical approach. We face now the claim that certain drugs can produce states indistinguishable from Christian mysticism, a claim that makes imperative, even if precarious, some distinction between Christian experience and Christian mysticism.[13]

Confusion arises from the fact that, for hundreds of years,

manuals on the spiritual life were written by monks and nuns who had a highly specialized vocation, part of which was to guide the spiritual growth of the laity. They were often spectacularly successful and, in the nature of the case, failures could be attributed to the irresponsible attitude of the lay person rather than to the methods of the director.

Let us recall Simone de Beauvoir's experience. In borrowing the *Handbook of Ascetic and Mystical Theology,* she was trying to find herself in terms of the approved method. The priest, too, attempted to locate her within the system. From both sides failure ensued, not because the spiritual directives were wholly at fault, but perhaps because the methods of mysticism are not universally applicable to those who wish to lead Christian lives.

Some persons are born activists. They can get from one point to another in their thinking without prolonged weighing of alternatives, interior debate, and extensive meditation. They do not have a mystical bone in their bodies. They sense where Christ is at work and, committed to discipleship, join him on that front. Others, on the contrary, cannot find their way through life without introspection and much meditation. Christian purpose cannot clarify and mature in them without contemplation. Spiritual leaders must take into account wide temperamental differences in human nature.

Sensitive clergy of all churches know this, but there is a factor that may be overlooked. One can have a passionate love for social and intellectual life *by temperament* and still have a burning desire for the highest possible communion with God. Those who use the manuals of the mystics, seeing this longing for God in an individual, may try to train it toward the vocation they think highest. Past generations saw this in the service of the church, but we must face the fact that an increasing number of persons see their vocation today in the world—in prison reform, legal aid to the poor, making government accountable to the people, and countless other places. Had Simone and her confessor been able to lay the manual aside and play the relationship by ear with God, this great woman might not have lost her faith.

What its loss may have meant to her cannot be determined from the outside, but it was certainly a sad loss for the church.[14]

The misunderstanding of sincere persons takes place in all communions, however, so let us now take an illustration from within Protestantism. As a minister and minister's wife, I deplored for years the cooking and serving of meals at the church. Surely women had enough of such activity at home, and the church should be able to guide them into a more significant supplementary ministry. If they could be moved, through study and prayer, to a clearer evaluation of their own gifts, would not the needs of Christian education, visits to the aging and ill, witness through movements and organizations other than the church be brought home to them? But one day it dawned on me that a fraction of women were finding their *mission* in the church kitchen. They were ministering to each other as they set tables and planned menus. Widows found healing for their loneliness in the fellowship of this larger family. Young and old were working together to hammer out a Christian philosophy of life. I stopped pressing for change that many did not want, and sought only the release of women who wished alternative opportunities for service.

Those who attend prayer groups occasionally bemoan the fact that the kitchen gets more feminine votes. Intercessory prayer, too, is work that must be done, though those on the outside may think of it as useless and sentimental. But does not our choice of work depend upon personality factors and natural gifts? It seems to me it has little or nothing to do with degrees of "spirituality"; the very word is offensive to modern ears. The striking difference between Christian experience and mystical experience is that, while we all have the same goal (love of God and fellowman), we are not all climbing the same ladder to get there.

An appreciation for the vocation of other persons can keep us from going to seed in our own. Mystical aspirations alone can pull a person so far out of the world that its tragedies are blurred. Most monasteries guard against this eventuality but, in recent years, many have felt that the walls were too much of a protection. Activists at the opposite extreme can be harnessed to so many carts that they forget what their merchandise is and for whom they are working.

In summary, all we live through in pursuing the twin goals of love of God and man counts as Christian experience. That this love is the truth about the meaning of life, we *presuppose* as followers of Jesus. It is not necessary to prove it; no one can prove a world view. The most we can do is to autograph our choice with our lives. Interests and temperament determine our particular *focus of attention*. The *change* brought about in us by Christ may be gradual or so rapid that others gaze with amazement. The *language* we use in sharing what means most to us will be influenced by the doctrines of our respective churches. But now we shall see how an entirely different type of experience may erupt in the Christian context.

Paranormal Experience

Paranormal experience, as the adjective suggests, refers to what happens on the fringe. Because the culture is pluralistic, though, average people are willing to move over and make room for all kinds of baffling phenomena, said to be observed by those on the outskirts of the normal. Up to the present generation, science has paid little attention to unusual happenings such as mental telepathy, precognition, clairvoyance, clairaudience, and alleged evidence for survival after death. It has been hard enough, too, for psychology to establish itself as a respectable science without letting parapsychology dog its steps, but at the end of 1969, the Parapsychological Association of America was admitted to the Society for the Advancement of Science.[15] This means little more than the recognition that there are border occurrences that, so far, have eluded explanation. Science cannot ignore them altogether unless it wants to be like the man who, late at night, kept circling a street light, looking for his keys. "Are you sure you lost them here?" a passerby inquired. "No," he answered, "but I can see better here." Both science and religion are naturally more comfortable in the light of established facts. The marginal poses a threat to what we think we already know.

My first real awareness of the paranormal came in seminary

when my roommate asked what I thought about the experience of a woman she knew who, as a high school girl, had wanted the lead in her class play more than she had ever wanted anything. Day after day, she stewed because there was one other girl with more talent who was likely to get the part. Finally her mother, exasperated, said, "Stop worrying! Mary is going to break her leg, and you will win." The prediction proved accurate, and the anxious mother told her daughter not to mention the remark, but the secret was more than the girl could bear. She had to tell a few friends: How did they think her mother knew? She wondered if her mother could have caused the accident in some mysterious way. My roommate's question upset a hornets' nest of theological problems in my mind. If such precognition is possible, what does it do to free will, to the meaning of time? Are future events laid out for us like a change of clothing so that we only put them on?

Unfortunately, I have no answer to these questions today, but there are two reasons why it is desirable to differentiate paranormal from Christian experience. First, the paranormal sometimes crops up in the experience of Christians and they try to find a religious meaning for it. Second, when scientific explanations can be made of cumulative evidence for supposedly unexplainable happenings, light may be thrown on the import of such Christian practices as prayer. Let us be clear about the latter. Christians will pray, with or without the sanctions of science, because they have been called to prayer by God. It would seem, though, they should welcome any findings that may possibly shed light on what happens in intercessory prayer. We shall return to this.

Let us look first at the paranormal as it intersects Christian experience. 1. Daniel Logan's Roman Catholic mother was distressed when he showed a tendency toward the psychic gifts of her father, a native of Czechoslovakia, who, employed by the New York City Transit Authority, possessed the peculiar power of telling at once whether claims against the Authority were fair or being faked for insurance money. He seldom missed. Now, in high school, Daniel himself became afraid that he might be demon-possessed. Where did he get this ability to tell which fellow would date a girl before either of them knew, and what had made him inform a friend that his parents would be divorced within a year? The boy had been indignant, insisting they got along well together, but Daniel's prediction came true. Still a young man, Daniel has come to believe that his gift can be exercised only when he is trying to help others. He thinks that the youth of the world can overcome hatred, war, selfishness, and even death.[16]

2. Edgar Cayce's parents took him to revival meetings as a boy and, by the time he was twelve years old, he had read the Bible through three times. Then, he began to say that he could see visions and that he could talk to relatives who had recently died. His parents thought he had an overactive imagination. But, as an adult, when he went into a sleep-like trance, he became able to diagnose the physical or mental illnesses of many persons who consulted him and to suggest remedies. His success, while not invariable, became spectacular enough that *The New York Times* carried two pages of headlines and pictures on October 9, 1910, and the University of Chicago, in 1954, accepted a Ph.D. thesis, based on his life and work. Cayce did not exploit his gifts for financial gain and, teaching a weekly Bible class, remained a conscientious and modest Presbyterian layman.[17]

3. Arthur Ford, whose family belonged to the Episcopal Church, first became aware of paranormal abilities when he was in the trenches during World War I. He would hear a voice informing him of the death of some soldier, and soon the name would appear on the casualty list. Ford came to believe that his psychic powers were a special gift that he could use for others. He was ordained to the ministry by the Disciples of Christ and felt called to combat the spirit of materialism in the world. He believed his mental and spiritual functions would go on without dependence upon his body.[18]

Logan, Cayce, and Ford, all born into Christian families, discovered their unusual gifts early in life, but are not such cases too rare to be worthy of mention? That question cannot be answered because science, dominating the culture, has looked askance at the paranormal, and those possessing such powers do not talk about them. But as is well known, people are often less guarded during illness, so I have questioned more than a dozen nurses: "Have you ever known personally (either in your own life, or in the life of someone close to you) of paranormal experience? (This would include precognition, telepathy, clairvoyance, clairaudience—any experience that seems to indicate communication with the unseen world or with the dead.)"

A registered nurse, Protestant and now retired, told me about a patient to whom she had long given private care and whose condition had changed little. One day, to her surprise, the woman patient asked that a male relative, employed in a city some distance away, be requested to come at once. The nurse demurred, saying that it would be easier for him to come over the weekend. "No," the patient replied, "send now. The Lord has told me that he will take me tonight." Thus pressed, the nurse complied, the relative came, and the woman died that night. How had she known? In what way did she think the Lord had spoken to her?

An elderly Roman Catholic nurse also had a strange story to tell. "I was sitting with a dying friend (also a nurse) when the patient suddenly said, 'Just a minute, Mother, when I cross this stream, I will be with you.' She lay back on her pillow and expired. Her mother had died six months before."

Younger nurses said that patients near death were often in a coma, had been given drugs to relieve pain, or were too weak to communicate, so they had no peculiar death-incidents to relate. Several mentioned, however, that there were often puzzling occurrences in the course of an illness, as, for example, a sudden unexpected recovery for which the physician could not account and that might have some paranormal explanation if all the facts were known. One nurse mentioned that a patient believed he had received a warning message through a dream, involving someone already dead.

Other nurses, both old and young, brushed the possibility of the paranormal aside, one saying that the past is more vivid to one dying than the present. She felt that supposedly psychic experience is only a revivification of the past, not a paranormal happening. A number of nurses were open to the possibility of telepathy and precognition, but rejected any thought of communication with the dead.

The commonest paranormal experience is probably that of dreams that seem to be conveying a meaning just beyond the dreamer's grasp. In this connection, let us look at Genie Price's recurrent dream of being in a tangled garden. A dream setting is often symbolic and, while symbols may differ from person to person, Edgar Cayce thought that a tangle usually suggested a need for cleansing. Freud had sought the meaning of dreams in the person's past, on the ground that they may indicate psychic illness; Jung looked to the future, believing they gave clues to wholeness. Both Freud and Jung, though in different senses, saw dreams as therapeutic.[19] It is interesting to note that when Eugenia Price wakened, she felt "all clean inside." There was no clue as to how this came about, but the climax of her dream had been the meeting with Ellen Riley who expressed delight in seeing her "back again." Did the dream, in some obscure way, motivate Genie to telephone Ellen, and did it prepare her for the renewal of friendship that brought about her conversion to Christ? And did someone's prayer have anything to do with it?

In his autobiography, Nicolas Berdyaev related what seemed to him a remarkable dream, prefiguring his spiritual pilgrimage. In the dream, he seemed to be in a huge square, looking for his place at a banquet that marked the beginning of an ecumenical council where important business was to be transacted, but whenever he tried to sit down, he was told that it was the wrong place, or that no place had been provided for him, although many of his Orthodox friends were present. Turning, he saw a large, rugged, bare rock at the very edge of the square and, going over to it, he began to climb, bruising his hands and feet, becoming utterly exhausted. Once he looked back and could see a winding, torturous road where others were struggling to ascend. Only the most agonizing effort enabled him to reach the top of the rock where suddenly he saw the figure of Christ crucified and fell at his feet, barely conscious.[20]

The dream stirred and shook Berdyaev, but did it have any meaning? Did it prepare him for the coming exile from his native Russia, an exile that nearly broke his heart, but at the same time, opened a way for wide and intensive communication with Christians of other communions? He says, "The moments of greatest inspiration were associated in my life with experiences evoked by dreams."

A student of Edgar Cayce's work, Harmon Hartzell Bro, thinks that dreams play a part in the life of prayer. Those that seem to have significance may come from the subconscious and help in problem-solving, or from the superconscious and tend to transformation.[21] The Bible records a number of incidents showing the antiquity of such dream experiences, and they are far from rare in modern times.[22]

We have seen that paranormal experience appears from time to time in the lives of Christians and may have significance for them. We come now to the question of what light continuing scientific studies may throw on the practice of prayer.

The controversy over extrasensory perception (ESP) erupted during the first quarter of this century when J. B. Rhine, who held a doctorate in biology, published an account of his experiments in the field of mental telepathy at Duke University. It was thought that anyone knows knowledge depends upon our five senses—seeing, hearing, handling, tasting, or smelling; these are the gateways through which the outside world reaches us. What, then, did a scientist mean by saying that contact could be made without the use of these senses? Frantically the educated world rummaged for proof that the known senses must have figured in his experiments in some way. When critics could find no fault with Dr. Rhine's experimental design or data analysis, they were so convinced that it is impossible for a person to guess correctly, out of all proportion to chance, the cards in the hand of someone in another room (for which evidence had been offered) that their presuppositions blinded them to facts.[23] There was no theory to account for what had been discovered and no conceptual framework to which it could be related. Decades of experimentation, however, have continued to indicate that there is some paranormal force in human experience that can even produce measurable physical change by extrasensory means. But parapsychology is still in its infancy, and basic theories related to such activity remain to be formulated.

Throughout his professional life, Sigmund Freud debated the meaning of thought-transference with his colleagues, trying to figure out where the truth lay. Several of them carried out experiments that turned out well, especially when Freud was the one analyzing his associations.[24] Psychoanalyst Ernest Jones, an English disciple and friend of Freud, constantly urged him to be more discreet in what he had to say on the subject. "I don't like it myself," Freud replied, "but there is some truth in it." Jones told him that ideas like that could lead to "beliefs in angels." "Quite so," Freud laughed, "and perhaps even in the Good Lord himself." Before his death, Freud commented that materialism faced a mystery and a secret. He felt that nothing had been proved about telepathy or clairvoyance, but believed such experiences more than accidental. He kept an open mind, saying, "All my life I have learned to accept new facts, humbly, readily."[25]

Between scientific experimentation and the spiritualistic medium with whom we associate occult practices, there is a vast no-man's-land. Daniel Logan noted that at least 75 percent of mediums he had seen who dealt in spiritualism turned out to be frauds or con men. However, he did not think the remaining 25 percent could be shrugged off. Samuel C. Soal, whose *Modern Experiments in Telepathy* was published by Yale University Press in 1954, attended as a psychic investigator a series of sittings with a medium, and reached the conclusion that the medium read the conscious or subconscious minds of the sitters in 90 percent of the cases; the rest remained a mystery.

H. Richard Neff, a Presbyterian pastor in Maryland, has made a careful study of ESP, prayer, healing, and survival, in which he tries to determine what is believable and what is not. Neff does not see psychic phenomena as "the work of the devil," but neither do they prove that "traditional Christian beliefs are true." Parapsychology, in his view, is a new frontier of human knowledge, in which there is some interpenetration of psychic events and religious experience that is not yet clear. New scientific developments should be of interest to persons with Christian faith, but they will not, of course, produce such faith.[26]

In the meantime, it is not advisable to try private experimentation with psychic phenomena. Ouija boards seem an innocent parlor game, but both Hugh Lynn Cayce, Edgar Cayce's son who runs a foundation based on his father's work and refers to himself as a "confused Presbyterian," and Richard Neff have known of mental trouble growing out of their use. As for automatic writing, I know a woman who became a victim, placing herself for hours at a time at the disposal of an "old Indian chief" who wanted to dictate to her. She recovered, but it was a frightening experience for her friends.

Persons distraught over the death of someone near to them may be tempted to try for communication through a medium, especially if a person they know well recommends it. More emotionally drained than they realize, and subjecting themselves to eerie phenomena, they may verge toward mental imbalance. A parishioner once consulted me about a terrifying experience she had had under such circumstances. The thing to remember is that psychic phenomena are neither good nor bad in themselves. When authentic, they cloak mystery, but God is far more likely to speak to our intelligence than to play hide and seek with us in spiritualistic seances. For reasons that I shall make clear in Part II, I believe the greatest comfort (strength and support) come to Christians through Holy Communion.

But let us go back to the question of mental telepathy, and, giving our imaginations free reign, let us consider the possibility that science may some day verify thought-transference and the conditions under which it is likely to occur. Let us entertain the further possibility that deep intercessory prayer may be found to be one such condition. What, if anything, would this suggest— that God is an illusion, that we can congratulate ourselves on a good deed when we pray for others? I think not. The fact that we are able to minister to each other's needs physically and materially does not surprise us. Why should we not be able to do the same thing mentally and spiritually once we learn how?

This says nothing whatever regarding the reality of God. We would simply have discovered a truth he tried to teach mankind throughout the years in which the Bible was coming into being, and has been teaching ever since to those who have faith to hear the message. If it becomes possible for science to tell us how thought-transference takes place, it will be explicating the human side of what has been enjoined upon us for centuries.

But there is a dark side to this picture that we must also consider. If seeking God's good gifts for others in prayer means that, in a sense, we are helping to deliver the things for which we ask, why should it not be possible for those who hate, also, to close their closet doors and wreak vengeance on their enemies? Moreover, would it not be possible for us to impose our own wills upon people in secret, dressing up the whole process prettily as God's design for them?

First of all, in intercessory prayer, we are never alone. If thought-transference occurs, Christians would still believe it to be within God's creative process. It has been said that our petitions are edited from the cross. This is highly symbolic language, but does it not mean that the nerve center of every prayer is divine love? Some fragment of divine love is the root of our prayer for others, the substance of its answer, and the medium of communication.

So, powerful as hate may be under certain conditions, Christians, presupposing a God of love rather than malevolence at the center of things, and focusing upon that love, do not fear any transference of evil from a human mind. Daniel Logan has been very conscious of this. He says:

It is remarkable that whenever a medium tries to use his gift for monetary gain or for other selfish purposes, the gift fails. This has been proved true not only in my own case, but in that of many famous mediums (Edgar Cayce, for example), some of whom I have known. It seems that it is only when the psychic's intention is to help others or enlighten them that the gift is operational.[27]

In opposition to Logan's point of view, it may be said that there are parts of the world where death is, in fact, caused by black magic. Missionaries who have lived a long time in cultures where this occurs confirm the truth of it, but this is due to fear, born of the presupposition that such transfer of calamitous purpose is possible and the focusing of attention on its coming. How often throughout the Bible is man, individually and collectively, told to "fear not"? It prefaces nearly every communication from a divine source.

In this chapter, I have shown that Christian experience flows through all the churches, with somewhat different colorings (doctrines) and channels (forms of expression). Mystics and activists live it out in different ways. It may coincide with a method or elude all methods. Not understanding some aspects of it, we may question their normality, but perhaps we do not yet see the length and breadth of what is normal when God and man meet.

It is to such a meeting in the life of one person that we turn in Part II.

Close-up of a
Christian Experience

CHAPTER 3

The Book That Covers a Voice

ALL EXPERIENCE IS PERSONAL AND UNIQUE, EVEN WHEN EMOTION and understanding fuse the feelings and perceptions about life held by two or more individuals. In these times of lightning change, moreover, all experience is quickly dated because of its sociological elements. What an older person has encountered may seem quaint, or even bizarre, to one born ten or twenty years later. Even those of the same generation with differing ethnic, economic, educational, and religious backgrounds, not to mention divergent temperaments or interests, may find it hard to speak a common language. Rigid and stereotyped sexual roles can place men and women in separate worlds.

But not always.

There are universals in experience that, shared, frequently melt ordinary human barriers and bring about unexpected rapport. One such meeting of minds occurred with Frank Laubach, whom I previously had not known. Nevertheless, he told me, "We have been through the same spiritual country." Sometimes, on the other hand, where we had expected mutuality, people shake their heads as though we had dropped from another planet— they have never seen the likes of us before.

So one can only be honest—and hope.

A Child's View of the Bible

A little book lover, I found the appearance of the Bible intriguing—heavy leather with gold lettering, pages that shone as it lay closed on the table. The deference paid to it in my grand-parents' home and at Sunday school roused curiosity as to what it contained, but when I asked my grandfather to buy a copy for me, his response was, "Read it, and I will." Church schools dis-tribute Bibles now to youngsters of a certain age; if they did so then, I was never in the right place at the right time to benefit.

The thought of starting to read the Bible any place except at the beginning never occurred to me, nor did anyone suggest an alternative approach. The first effort carried me well into Deu-teronomy, where I lost heart. A year or so later, during summer vacation, I made a fresh start and kept afloat until grounded on the shoals of 1 Chronicles. It was all so hard to grasp. "What is circumcision?" I asked my grandmother.

"Look it up in the dictionary."

"What is a foreskin? It says here 'to cut off the foreskin of,' and what does this mean, 'and he came in unto her and she con-ceived'?" My grandmother, an honest and sensible person, gave me minimal sex information.

The Bible has never been a magic book to me, nor a fetish, and I attribute this to the sheer horror of incidents like those recorded in the nineteenth chapter of Judges. Such sickening brutality made me shudder from head to foot. The absence of saccharine sweetness and shimmering light may have helped to prepare me for the appreciation of words I was to find later.

Paul's Inexhaustible World View

Then, at the age of fourteen, as I have already related, came the shattering blow of my mother's death and the first awareness of the church as an entity. For, although my father was not a member, he knew intuitively the woman who would respond to our call for help in the middle of the night. Mrs. Bair came and stayed until relatives arrived. When it was decided that what was left of our family would remain together, she and other church women tried in practical ways to be mothers to me. Mrs. Bair gave me a New Testament in which she had written a short note: "My dear girl, as you read the precious words within this book, I pray that your young life will be blessed. May your light so shine before men, that they may see your good works, and glorify your Father which is in heaven. Matthew 5:16."

Although my grandfather, impressed with my efforts, had given me a Bible of my own, progress through the Old Testament was slow. I still had not finished it. This New Testament was much easier to read.

One night I had a peculiar dream, one of two in my life that possibly had some significance. We were still living in the country, and I dreamed of walking diagonally across an open field with the apostle Paul. He was a slight, dark-complexioned man with animated face and large, expressive eyes. Entranced with his words, I forgot to watch where I was going, and nearly fell into a gully, but he caught my elbow and steadied me. When we reached the fence, he vanished, and I wakened with a feeling of exaltation that evaporated immediately because I could not bring to mind a single word he had said.

Some days later, however, when the dream, having no special message, had been forgotten, and I was reading Paul's letter to the Philippians, I came upon the words, "Let this mind be in you, which was also in Christ Jesus." Suddenly the dream flashed back with tremendous force, accompanied by the certainty, "This is what Paul said; it is all he really said; every word he spoke was related to these." Needless to say, the message sank in.

All the young people liked Mrs. Bair, who taught our Sunday school class. She was outgoing and had a delightful sense of humor. One lesson, in particular, spoke to me. It had to do with the transmission of the prophetic message from Elijah to Elisha upon the former's death. Elijah had asked his follower if he had any request to make, and Elisha replied, "I pray thee, let a double portion of thy spirit be upon me (2 Kings 2:9, KJV)." The story reveals the difficulty, but the request was granted, and symbolized by Elisha's assuming Elijah's mantle. The incident remained in my thoughts and led me to ask Mrs. Bair one day if she would let her mantle fall on me when she died. The idea struck her as hilarious, but when she saw I was serious, she said, keeping a straight face, "I will if I can." This was of more than passing importance.

Probably most high school students, from time to time at least, have longer thoughts than they are given credit for. One of mine was: what can a person believe? A girl friend was all wrapped up in H. G. Wells's writing; she would have accepted anything he said. The books of Ephesians, Philippians, and Colossians appealed to me, but a special point penetrated. It is expressed in Colossians 2:2-4, and is to the effect that all the treasures of wisdom and knowledge are in God the Father and in Christ. "Unless a person wants to be a cork on an ocean," I thought, "he has to stand somewhere, have some point of view from which to evaluate everything that happens to him, and my point of view is going to be Christ." I adopted this teaching of Paul[1] as my presupposition about life, not that I had a neat, succinct conception of Christ; the apostle had said his full meaning was a mystery. It certainly was to me, and has remained so, but the decision was the taking of a direction.

The Coming of the Presence

In a tactful way, and without embarrassing anyone, Mrs. Bair encouraged us to express ourselves, and, occasionally, to voice a short prayer. This was hard, but it did create a sense of belonging. Then, as I have said, our family moved back to the city. Wrenched away from friends, I struggled to pray, reading daily from both the Old and New Testaments.

One night, a deep stillness, foreign to the noisy street where we lived, came over me. Enveloped in silence, some power wordlessly questioned me, and my mind floundered for language with which to reply. "I can't preach," I breathed. And then words came from the other, "I am not looking for someone who can preach, but for someone who will speak my words." The Presence asked obedience, not ability and, overcome with awe, I tried to make an affirmative response with no resource except willingness. I had never heard of a woman minister. Mrs. Bair had what Methodists called an "exhorter's license," but I never, then or later, associated the kind of leadership she gave with preaching. As far as I know, she never went into the pulpit. There was nothing in my previous experience to account for such an audacious notion.

But a few days later, as I was reading the book of Isaiah, a sentence seemed to leave the page and become a promise made to me personally. It was: "I will go before thee, and make the crooked places straight: I will break in pieces the gates of brass, and cut in sunder the bars of iron: And I will give thee the treasures of darkness, and hidden riches of secret places, that thou mayest know that I, the Lord, which call thee by thy name, am the God of Israel (Isa. 45:2-3, KJV)." To my mind, the words promised that God would take the initiative in my life. I would find and know him in all the hard and dark places; he would be ahead of me, awaiting discovery everywhere.

Now, any good Bible student knows that the words mean nothing of this kind. They were addressed to neither Jew nor Christian, but to King Cyrus of Persia, and the victory promised was earthly as were the treasure and riches. The words had not conveyed the author's meaning at all, but they had become a vehicle for God's word to me. I had not been straining to hear the divine voice. Such a procedure in prayer or Bible reading can activate the imagination to an alarming extent, and there is no telling what weird fancies may result. I had not, in fact, taken any initiative in the matter and, aside from the incident of the dream I have related, it was the first time the Bible had ever projected a personal message to me. I took what the words communicated as a factual assurance from God himself.[2]

In an interview with Ingmar Bergman, Lewis Freedman quotes the playwright as saying, "I always have been interested in these voices inside you. . . . I think everybody hears these voices and those forces."[3] He had always wanted to accord them the status of fact, not to treat them as "unreal imaginings but to treat them as facts, and therefore to relate to them in a serious way." This is what I did, and I think it is the reason the experience set the tone for my life.

Adolescence, however, is a time of high mountains and low valleys. There was constant tension in our family, and I always had the feeling that unless I hung on to faith for dear life, I would lose it. This attitude may have come from a picture that fascinated me as a very small child. It was a stormy scene of wild sky and turbulent waves. In the center one could make out a stone cross, and to it a frightened girl with long, streaming hair was clinging precariously. I think the title of the picture was "Rock of Ages."

It is never easy for a young person to adjust to living without a mother. My father had married an attractive woman, ten years my senior and thirteen years his junior. While he had prepared us adequately for this event, and had even gone through the formality of making sure that it was acceptable to me, I proved unable to put another woman in my mother's place, especially a woman nearer my own age than my father's. I could not get used to my new role except by withdrawal, and one night in prayer, said, "I can't hold on any longer; I am going to let go. I can't be a Christian."

The response was warm and immediate: "I have been waiting for you to do that. You think you will fall but you will not. I will catch you." The quick answer was unexpected, but a few days later, I saw in Deuteronomy the words that gave added assurance to what I had heard, "The eternal God is thy refuge, and underneath are the everlasting arms (Deut. 33:27, KJV)."

By the time I had reached the middle of the Old Testament, in addition to its inspiring passages, I had come upon a number of revolting stories that disclosed the depths to which human sexual relations can descend. But, almost unbelievably, the Song of Solomon conveyed no erotic meaning whatever. This was probably due to the synopsis that preceded each chapter in the King James version of the Bible, indicating a wholly allegorical interpretation—the mutual love of Christ and his church. There was no way of telling that they were not part of the original. Scholars are not sure how this book got into the Bible and stayed there, but the likely explanation lies in the supposed authorship of Solomon and its symbolical significance. Modern scholars conjecture that it may be a drama, a collection of secular love songs, a Syrian wedding ritual, or a Hebrew poem, showing the influence of a Canaanite liturgy of the god and goddess of fertility.[4]

Never having heard of such hypotheses, I approached the requests in this book as prayers that might suitably be offered to Christ by any member of his church; the affirmations were divine promises. Even as a child, I had had no mental images of God, nor did the use of masculine pronouns suggest a male being. (I find the use of female pronouns for God, as a corrective to male chauvinism, unfortunate because they drag sex in and make an issue of it where it has no relevance at all; to my way of thinking, God is not both male and female—he is beyond sex.)

When I came to the fourteenth verse of the second chapter of the Song of Solomon, containing the words, "Let me see thy countenance, let me hear thy voice; for sweet is thy voice, and thy countenance is comely," they seemed to make prayer for a vision of Christ quite legitimate. Using these words, I prayed with great intensity and expectation one evening for their fulfillment. Nothing happened, so I prayed more earnestly, not because I needed proof of divine reality,[5] but because love craved sight. There was no response, my energy was running out, but I felt impelled to go on praying when, all at once, the prayer seemed to be receiving outside support and amplification. Suddenly I became aware of a localized Presence entering the darkness of the room from its northeast corner. (I do not know whether this direction would have meaning for any religious group or not, but that is the way the Presence came.) I saw nothing, heard nothing, touched nothing, but the Presence was approaching and sustaining me in the approach. I felt only one emotion—adoration. There was no feeling of hurry, but after a time, the Presence withdrew as it had come. I walked on air for days. It was years, however, before I knew that a great gift had been left. I would never be able to conceive of ultimate reality in any terms except that Presence; in that one experience, I had known what reality is.

Probably the heaviest burden of adolescence is its fluctuating emotion. I was sixteen, and life at home was miserable, as it often is for persons that age. A further factor that I shall mention later complicated my existence. Loneliness grew and fostered the feeling that no one cared for me. This was not true, but once a person gets that idea, it is hard to dislodge. He reaches out for understanding, and meets nothing but cold walls. An occasional trip to our former community kept me going, and a family there, the Kitzmillers, never failed to make me feel welcome for a weekend. The lonesomeness nevertheless increased, and one night, in dejection and self-pity, I opened the Bible to where I was reading in Jeremiah; it happened to be the thirty-first chapter and, in a moment, I came upon the words, "The Lord hath appeared of old unto me, saying, Yea, I have loved thee with an everlasting love; therefore with loving kindness have I drawn thee." That love lifted, enveloped, and reassured me.

A year or so later, I came across a poem of Frances Ridley Havergal that described my feeling perfectly, although the writer belonged to a past generation:

The human heart asks love,
But now I know that my heart hath from Thee
All real, and full, and marvelous affection,
So near, so human, yet divine perfection
Thrills gloriously the mighty glow.
Thy love is enough for me.[6]

Then less than a year ago, in a wholly different setting, I found the experience related again by Piri Thomas who prayed in the Bronx Tombs, "plain . . . like a little kid," expressing his wants, lacks, hopes, and disappointments, confessing his "blanks," and asking for God's help and friendship. "I began to feel better inside," he says, "like God had become Pops and Moms to me. I felt like I was someone that belonged to somebody who cared. I felt like I could even cry if I wanted to, something I hadn't been able to do for years."[7] God's love is trans-generational; only the way of putting it in words changes.

Decisions

A first year in college was made possible by my grandfather and a great uncle. They had wanted me to go to nearby Heidelberg College in Tiffin, Ohio, but I was able to win their reluctant permission to attend Taylor University in Indiana instead. The atmosphere there, charged with religion, suited me perfectly for more than a year.

But I found that I did not want to study the Bible and theology in college. My relatives, having little faith in a woman's ability to earn her living in a religious profession, were urging me to qualify to teach in both Indiana and Ohio. This called for many courses in education, as well as in major subjects, leaving few electives. I had come under the influence of B. W. Ayres, who was vice-president of the university and taught philosophy. I had the good fortune to be his secretary during the summer months when he dictated one shorthand notebook after another to former students in every part of the world who sought his point of view on innumerable controversial issues. He gave his opinion fully, simply, modestly, often telling those in graduate work that they were in closer touch with developing thought than he was, and expressing confidence in their judgment. The letters sometimes ran to several closely typed pages, and I knew they would be cherished for years by the recipients and would likely be a major influence in their decision-making as, later, they were to become in mine. If his secretary was not available, Dr. Ayres wrote the letters by hand, beautifully readable even after he became an octogenarian. I had to choose between philosophy and theology, and chose the former.

The fundamentalist atmosphere at Taylor had been congenial and when I learned, at the beginning of my senior year, that I had been accepted as a student at Hartford Theological Seminary, and awarded one of the two scholarships available to entering women through the kindness of the Woman's Board, I took careful stock. Anticipating that the transition to a liberal seminary might be quite a jolt, I tried to work through my beliefs and to determine, ahead of time, which were most important. Under the influence of the apostle Paul, I sought to fathom the mind of Christ, and settled upon love of God and faith in him as Jesus' central concern. The other essential was love for human beings and the desire that they might know God. On all other points, I would be flexible. My last sermon to my homiletics class at seminary was based on the words, "Let this mind be in you which was also in Christ Jesus," and the professor, Rockwell Harmon Potter, told me, "What you learned before you came to Hartford is more important than anything you have found out here."

G. H. C. MacGregor's critical, exegetical approach to the Bible was balanced by courses on its use in teaching and preaching, taught by Alexander Purdy, a Quaker.[8] "Wee MacGregor's" Commentary on the Gospel of John in the Moffatt series had been harshly criticized as leaving that book "a broken and dismembered corpse." This cut him to the core, as he handled biblical revelation with utmost reverence. One day he inquired of a class, "Do you think Jesus meant to teach so-and-so by this passage?" "I don't know," a bright student replied, "but if he did, I think he was wrong." The small, mild professor leaped from behind the lectern and thundered, "No one shall speak of Jesus Christ in that way in this class." The student apologized. The same profound scholarship, coupled with deep Christian humility, prevailed in theology courses. "When I leave your class, I always feel as though I have been in church," I told Herbert H. Farmer. "I have never received a finer compliment," was his reply. The expected shake-up in a liberal seminary had not come, possibly because the Bible itself influenced me more than what others, liberal or conservative, said about it.

Reading the Bible with Children

Upon finishing seminary, I married a classmate, and after a year in northern Maine, we went to Montana where our two sons were born. When they outgrew *Thoughts About God for Boys and Girls*, I began reading the New Testament to them in consecutive fashion. This was with their full approval because it meant they would have my undivided attention at bedtime which, with any luck, they could postpone by questions and discussion.

Speaking frequently to groups of young mothers on the subject "Religion in the Home," I asked our boys' advice: "Do you think I ought to suggest that they read the Bible aloud to their children, or is it too hard to understand?" They reflected; then Bricker, the older one, said, "Romans and Hebrews were too hard to understand, but not the rest." He was starting junior high at the time.

"How about the Revelation?" I asked. "Surely that was rough going."

"Oh, no," he answered. "That was better than any comic book." The remark was not flippant, but the highest praise he could give.

We read several Old Testament books together, too. Once in Psalms, they burst into uproarious laughter for no reason that I could see. We had just read Psalm 7:16, "His mischief returns upon his own head, and his violent dealing shall come down upon his own pate." "I didn't know the Bible had slang in it," one of the boys said; "It struck me so funny—*pate*." The word occurs nowhere else in the scriptures, and the dictionary says that the term, meaning "top of the head," may be humorous or derogatory.

David liked such biblical fiction as *Beggar Boy of Galilee*.[9] Three years younger than his brother, he could not follow the Bible reading as easily, but once, when we were rereading, during Lent, the account of Jesus' last week, he said, "Whew, that was a great story."

"Why, David," I exclaimed with surprise, "you sound as though you had never heard it before."

"I never did," was his reply.

Relevance of the Bible for Adults

When our boys left home, and my husband's work, nearly always requiring his evenings, now involved considerable travel covering three states for the conference, my home Bible study again became private. As one becomes familiar with the books in their entirety, new levels of meaning open up. The average secular book can be grasped in a single reading; a few will bear a second or third perusal; we return to the great ones for years; but the Bible yields its import slowly through life-long meditation. The early Christians delighted in Old Testament studies long before there was a New Testament. With joy and excitement their leaders discovered the roots of what they had experienced in Christ.

But there is a dismal side to the Bible too. What are we to make of commands to destroy whole cities, to kill all the men as well as the married women and children, to treat single women as lustful soldiers will?[10] It is easy enough to understand this if we regard the Bible as dealing with raw human nature, undergoing the education of God over a period of centuries, but is it not somewhat misleading to refer to the whole library, without differentiation, as "the Word of God"? Does this not imply that these words, in distinction from all others, come from God? Fundamentalist leaders, making extensive use of the Bible, unconsciously slide over the difficulty, valuing in practice some parts much more than others, but not wanting to deny the divine origin of any part. Liberal churches say quite frankly that the Bible *contains* the Word of God, allowing portions that seem unlike him in the light of Jesus' teaching to fall into disuse. But the unavoidable inference here is that one may be selective and choose what sounds God-like, dismissing whatever seems untenable. We have, then, the absolute attitude of conservatives that leaves no room for selectivity and the relative attitude of liberals that makes God's word a matter for individual judgment, some of which, to say the least, is not very enlightened. There is, also, the Catholic position that restricts those who have the right to interpret.

In what sense does the Bible carry revelation from God that can be a guide to those who read it now? Biblical theology has fallen upon hard times because this question remains unsolved. The problem for conservatives, as I see it, is: How are we to interpret passages that command, in the name of God, what is now considered immoral action by any civilized person, if we insist that the whole Bible is, literally, the inspired "Word of God"? The corresponding question for liberals is: Since the understanding of the Bible requires highly specialized study for which lay persons have not the preparation, time, or attraction, how can they be expected to take an interest in reading it? Traditionally, the

Catholic Church has not encouraged individual Bible reading by
its members. (Scripture permeates the liturgy, and the homily
usually offers an interpretation.) But this attitude is changing,
and the encouragement of lay persons to study is battling long
generations of passive acceptance.

Unless these issues can be faced together, it seems to me that
there is little point in trying to keep the Bible as the dynamic
center of our religious heritage, and if we discard it, or banish
it to the fringe, we then face the still more stupendous problem:
what do we put into the place of from twelve to fifteen hundred
years of meaningful testimony as to what man has learned from
God? For that is about the length of time it took the Bible, as
we know it, to come into being. Are we not rootless enough as it
is? Where do we go for spiritual direction?

Apropos of this point, Arthur A. Cohen tells a story about
prayer that has come down to the Jewish people through a
Hasidic master, but may have meaning for Christians, too, as we
consider what has happened to our use of the Bible:

When the Baal Shem Tob, the founder of Hasidism had been
alive, he would go each day to a certain place in the forest, light
there a fire, and say his prayers; his successor knew the place in
the forest and remembered to light the fire, but no longer
remembered the Baal Shem's prayer, and *his* successor no
longer knew the place and could no longer light the fire; and he
in his generation, all that he could do was to tell the story.[11]

"The point is," continues Cohen, "that in our time we no longer
even have the enthusiasm to tell the story, believing perhaps that
even the story has become meaningless." In this connection,
James D. Smart, in *The Strange Silence of the Bible in the
Church*, shows how the problem we now face has developed and
its dimensions.[12]

Because the Bible has both chilled my blood with horror, and
also revealed the word of God to me, I have wrestled with this
problem throughout my adult life: how shall we approach the
Bible today?

There are two ways of working toward a solution: 1. We may use the critical methods that try to get at the biblical author's intention and the situation in which he found himself. This requires facility with ancient languages, a background in early Semitic and other history, knowledge of archaeological discoveries, to say nothing of the literary forms involved. Clearly, no one without proper academic competence can make a contribution from this angle. There cannot, however, be too much of this kind of critical study that deepens scholarly appreciation of what the Bible offers. A scientific discipline, it is subject to the limitations of science, and may or may not be combined with the second method to be mentioned, that of contemplative study.

2. There can be, and has been, too little contemplative study of the Bible, where the searcher for God prays and tries, with the help of the Holy Spirit, to learn his will as it has been revealed to mankind in the past. It is this second approach, in which any sincere person may share, that concerns us here. We will consider four aspects of it.

The Contemplative Reading of the Bible

1. The person who reads the Bible in contemplative fashion can expect epiphanies from time to time. This means that the modern seeker after truth can look forward to the showing forth of God's own light from the scriptures. The only requirement is that he became a disciplined searcher; there is no prerequisite of age, native intelligence, nor education. The Holy Spirit meets every individual where he is, not in some specially designed place that he must first reach by arduous efforts. I once heard a story about a mentally retarded man who was in deep trouble. He had the idea that the Bible is a kind of magic answer book and, if he would open it and put his finger on a page, he would find what he needed. Raising his finger, he found it had covered the words, "It came to pass." "That doesn't mean anything," he thought, "I'll try again." A second time he found the same words, but they still said nothing to him. "The third time will be the charm," he encouraged himself, "so I'll try once more." The same words again; they occur often in the Authorized Version of

the Old Testament. He thought as hard as he could, and then his face lighted up. "Of course, this trouble came to *pass*," he beamed. "It didn't come to stay. God will bring me through." For him, this was an epiphany. The person who is not mentally deficient is unlikely to get help of this kind, for God accommodates himself to limitations, not to spiritual laziness. When I read the scriptures consecutively, day after day, in my early teens, they puzzled me, shocked me, were too hard, but then, time and time again, as I have shown, some marvelously revealing light fell upon my way.

Let us note one more illustration before we leave this point. A kind, motherly woman from the deep South, who did prison work with men who were little more than boys, related the following incident. The warden had asked her to try to talk with a very young fellow who refused to say a word to anyone. When he was brought in, she was overcome with emotion because of his remarkable resemblance to her favorite nephew. Tears filled her eyes and she could think of nothing to say, so they sat in silence. Before leaving, she gave him a New Testament with Psalms and, pointing to the latter, said, "Read here, and I feel sure God will help you." Upon her return, a week or so later, his face shone. He opened to the psalms and pointed to the verse that had been an epiphany for him.

Mental assent to the church's teaching that the Bible is inspired means little unless it illuminates our own experience and inspires us. What the words meant when they were written centuries ago is important to scholars, and to ourselves indirectly, but, from time to time, God will bring some special meaning home to any prayerful individual. One of the things that makes the biblical message durable is the fact that its significance is pluriform, that is, it can address countless persons at widely separated historical and geographical locations, guiding and enlightening them in terms they can grasp, not all at once but in a growing, cumulative way. Its meaning is as manifold as the number of genuine readers.[13]

2. But the Bible does more than bring us to epiphanies. It initiates a conversation with us. Again and again, the divine

Presence questions us as it did those who first heard the message. Moses was asked, "What is that in your hand (Exod. 4:2)?" Amos—"What do you see (Amos 7:8)?" Jonah—"Do you do well to be angry (Jonah 4:4)?" The disciples on the road to Emmaus—"What is this conversation which you are holding with each other as you walk (Luke 24:17)?" There are many other examples, but the Presence wants to hear, too, what *we* have to say. The late Rabbi Abraham J. Heschel says, "In a sense, prophecy consists of a revelation of God and a *co-revelation of man*."[14] The prophets were not "recording instruments," neither were they persons whose insight came from their own strength and labor.[15] The prophet grew, wrestled, and prayed. Inspiration and experience mingled. God spoke; he answered. God revealed; he reacted. This process is repeated, to some extent, in every individual who hears God speaking to him through the sacred writings.

3. Amos Wilder has remarked that when epiphany is powerful, it orders reality.[16] One cannot be in conversation with the living God and go along as though nothing were happening. He accepts us as we are. This has been said so often that it may obscure its sequel: He does not leave us as we are. He influences us, helping us to become the fully developed followers of Christ we are called to be. This involves *change* that is sometimes very painful. If there is no tension in which God is summoning us to higher levels of action, the chances are we are not yet hearing the divine voice. I well remember the struggles I had as a teen-ager on the question of truthfulness. Other young persons have told me of similar bouts with God. He is not a yes-man who always pats us approvingly on the back, but he is patient and kind, as well as firm, in disciplining us.

One of our favorite methods of self-defense is to postpone change—"Later, Lord; I don't think the time is ripe," we argue, when we see a difficult job that should be done. James T. Burtchaell tells of a professor of classics who used to discuss in his classes "the principle of unripe time" which is "that people should not do at the present moment what they think right at that moment, because the moment at which they think it right has

not yet arrived," adding indelicately, "Time . . . is like the med-
lar; it has a trick of going rotten before it is ripe."[17]

The Bible does not save us the trouble of spiritual ventures of
our own. It registers soundings, puts down markers, and enables
us to chart our way out into the immensity of personal en-
counters with God. Eugenia Price says, "The Word became
flesh, not printer's ink, and as glorious as is that Spirit-inspired
account of God's divine nature and plan, its light is to me the
person of my Lord, Jesus Christ."[18] As the living Christ goes
ahead, he changes our presuppositions, our focus of attention,
and the very language we use.

4. So far, we have been seeing the contemplative reading of
the Bible as an individual matter, but one is not likely to read far
or long by himself. While in the twentieth century, we may make
our personal responses, we shall soon discover that we are not
traveling alone. Whether we read in the Old or New Testament,
we are made aware of a community to which, as seekers of God,
we belong. We are not being given special escort on separate,
private pilgrimages. We are en route with numberless others on
some vast, and often incomprehensible (to us), mission of the
divine Presence in this world. As Cohen says, the Bible "becomes
transitive."[19] It links the experience of those who sought God in
the past to his future purposes through the company of persons
now alert to his leading in the world. The scriptures through
which the church hears the voice of God are not merely archives
of the past but a vehicle in which God is continually coming to
his people.[20] Promises look to fulfillment, though generations pass
before hope materializes. "The government shall be upon his
shoulder (Isa. 9:6, KJV)," Isaiah wrote of the one we call Christ
and we presuppose, in God's time, it will be, and proceed as
faithfully as we can.

The Bible always calls us beyond the current culture. When
man in ancient times would kill the one who injured him, the
divine command was, "An eye for an eye, and a tooth for a
tooth"[21]—no more. It was still normal to hate your enemies. Man
could not learn everything in a few generations. But when Jesus
came, he proclaimed, "You have heard that it was said to the

men of old . . . but I say to you, . . ."[22] and he went on to give his teaching that we are to love even our enemies as God loves them. Whenever the divine word is heard through the Bible, it challenges cultural assumptions, so no one should ever ransack this holy book for ammunition to defend the status quo.

There is good to accept and bad to reject in every social order, including our own, but once we ally ourselves with those who seek God, we participate in a culture that stretches far back beyond the countries of our family origin, through Palestine with its humiliating cross, all the way to Abraham who heard the call to strike out for a new world, armed with faith in God. This culture reaches forward, too, toward the unforeseeable future when "The kingdom of the world [shall] become the kingdom of our Lord and of his Christ (Rev. 11:15)," and not until that day shall have arrived, however God brings it, can the divine word and the cultures of man be at perfect peace with one another.

There is a biblical world view that unveils itself slowly to the modern searcher for God. It has nothing to do with a "three story universe"—heaven, earth, hell—or with the length of time it took the world to come into existence, or with any other scientific question. It has to do with the centrality of God and man's call to worship him and learn from him. This is what Paul saw, and one can be receptive to the discoveries of each new century and share his world view.

But is this not an outburst of faith rather than a calm assessment of the possibilities? An answer to that question will depend upon presuppositions, our focus of attention, the direction in which we are moving, and the realm of discourse in which we feel comfortable. Final solutions are not in sight.

CHAPTER 4

That One Talent

THE PLACE OF PREACHING IN TODAY'S WORLD IS PROBLEMATIC.
How do ministers themselves regard this function? How important is it to the congregation? If people expected a "word from
the Lord," would they skip public worship for trivial reasons,
for mystical communion with nature, on any pretext? If there
is no "word from the Lord," how can a minister justify his role
in the pulpit as anything more than imparting religious information or good advice? Eric Sevareid remarked recently that
"preachers make the rest of us feel underdoggy." For that matter, why cannot a person do his own preaching to himself? As
ministers recognize, the indifference of many lay persons could
lie in the inadequacy of the pulpit. It could also lie elsewhere as,
for example, in loss of faith in a God who has nothing to say
to man. There is no one answer.

This chapter will show how my vocation to ministry developed
both prior to and within the context of marriage.

A Call from the Heights—or Depths

At the age of fifteen, two things seemed clear regarding my
future vocation: I was to "speak God's words," an activity that I
assumed meant preaching, and I would not have to chop my way
through to opportunities; they would open up. Then, as now, the
idea of uttering a more than human word was sobering. I never
conceived it in terms of personal authority, nor did I think for
one moment that some divine seizure would bring from my lips
words that had not been in my own mind.

But I did believe that listening prayer brought the inspiration for a sermon and that the thoughts grew out of an initiative not my own. My part was to speak what I heard with integrity, and not merely to pass on what I had read in a periodical or book. Would God summon us to a task, I reasoned, and then give no inkling of what we are to do? He wants truthfulness in his followers, based on wholehearted attention and response to him. But even so, can a minister deliver a package of *truth*? In the beginning I was naive enough to think this possible.

My first invitation to speak from a pulpit came before I had finished high school, the summer between my junior and senior years. It was offered by the Evangelical Church in Fostoria, Ohio, of which an uncle was a member. During vacations, I was active with the youth of that church, and they knew I planned to be a minister. In preparation and prayer, my mind was drawn to Jesus' words, "Have faith in God." Quiet meditation brought thoughts thick and fast. The congregation, swelled by my Methodist relatives who were torn between pride and anxiety lest I disgrace the family, was pleased. One member of the church, with more enthusiasm than common sense, said, "I wish you were our pastor."

My home church in Canton, Ohio, of which I shall have more to say in the next chapter, was small enough for the minister to be alert to individual needs. Young persons were seen as responsible participants in all that the congregation was doing. It was normal for us to contribute insights when parts of the Bible were under discussion, to take office, and to give liberally from whatever income we might be receiving. The advice to Timothy was taken seriously: "Let no man despise thy youth; but be thou an example of the believers, in word, in conversation, in charity, in spirit, in faith, in purity (1 Tim. 4:12, KJV)."

When the church, knowing my future commitment, licensed me to preach, it was without my request or knowledge. I was simply given a certificate, indicating the action, and, soon afterward, was invited to preach a sermon. Members of the congregation had heard me speak at small gatherings. Elated by this new opportunity, I forgot the essence of what had been my call to the ministry. In civics class at school, we had been studying the functions of government. What a coincidence, then, to discover in Isaiah the words, "The Lord is our judge, the Lord is our lawgiver, the Lord is our king; he will save us (Isa. 33:22, KJV)." Here, in the Old Testament, the government of God was proclaimed as a judicial, legislative, and executive function. I had only to combine the scripture with our American system— and there was the sermon!

To say that it was a flop is an understatement; to a sensitive teen-ager, it was a disaster. After the service, one of the less tactful women inquired, "What, exactly, was it you were trying to say?" The minister was kind, and gave no hint of his disappointment. Going home, I said, "This is the end; I will never preach again." But the Presence promised, with no imperative implied, "You will preach again and again and again, but never again as you did tonight." The realization of how competent I had felt was a continuing humiliation. Later, our minister gave me *A Treatise on Homiletics* from his library.

After a postgraduate semester in high school, and a short, but thorough secretarial course at a business college, I enrolled, as I have said, at Taylor University in Upland, Indiana, where chances to do gospel-team work were immediately offered. On the invitation of local churches in the vicinity, several young persons would go out to lead morning or evening worship. Usually the women sang and the men preached. Sometimes the men provided special music, but it was rare for a woman to speak, except in personal testimony. Few of those preaching had the resources to take twenty minutes so it was customary for two to speak. I cannot remember a single instance when my male preaching partner was unhappy about sharing the pulpit with a woman, nor can I recall raised eyebrows among ministers or congregations. The first money I ever received for preaching was five dollars from a local Friends Meeting. One of the leading men gave me the check, and an aged woman asked, "My dear girl, what is thee going to do with thy life?"

With the encouragement of a seminary scholarship, and a loan of less than a hundred dollars from my grandfather to clear my remaining college debt, it was possible to continue my education without interruption. There was mild surprise at seminary that a woman was planning to preach; most of the small number of women students were expecting to teach in college, or to go to the mission field. Faculty and students alike, however, took my purpose seriously and did not make me feel out of place. As outside work (now called field work), I taught two classes of junior high girls, one a paid position in a wealthy downtown church, the other in a mission where most of the pupils were from minority groups. Once I entertained the two classes together on the seminary grounds. If any parents, delivering or picking up their children, were shocked at seeing the two groups together, they kept their opinions to themselves.

Women in seminary now might want to ask the question: "If student pastorates were available, why were you not given one of them? Why were you teaching in church school?" Not all the men who wanted to fill pulpits had the opportunity, but there was a very good reason, apart from sex, why it did not come my way. Student pastors were in small, out-of-town churches and one had to have a car, whatever its stage of decrepitude. I did not consider trying to get one and learning to drive, however, because I was extremely nearsighted, had only 20-10 vision in both eyes, and was color-blind; red and black looked the same to me. Moreover, my eyes were abnormally sensitive to light. Any degree of natural light affected them in the same way that going out of a totally dark room into brilliant sunshine would affect others. This eye condition had led the dean of my college to tell me, firmly but kindly, just before graduation, that I could never hope to teach or preach for a living. His desire to fortify me against future disappointment knocked the bottom out of my world until the Presence said, "He did not call you; trust me."

Marriage

Although my preaching was accepted without question by men at college, as well as by women, they almost never asked me for dates. The thought of marriage had not occurred to me, and I am sure did not occur to any of them in connection with a person like me. Seminary, however, was different. I began dating right

away and married a classmate four years later, after receiving
the Bachelor of Divinity and Master of Sacred Theology degrees.
There was not the slightest thought, when I married, that I was
rejecting my own call to ministry; we were simply joining forces.
I did not, however, expect to serve as co-pastor with my husband.[1]
Basically, my long-standing attitude had been to leave the initiative to God. Marriage seemed a natural, normal development in
life. I foresaw no conflict.

But having been enclosed by academic walls for eight years, I
had lost all realization of what it takes in time to keep a house
attractive, and had not the least idea of what the attitude of a
local church toward the ministry of a woman might be. This was
incredibly naive. The church, as usual, called my husband, and
got me for free. At the time, neither I nor anyone else questioned
the justice of this.

The first year was frustrating because it looked as though I
were to have no opportunity for ministry at all beyond teaching
a Bible course at the high school. My husband's attitude saved
the day because he recognized more clearly than I did, in the
beginning, that it was essential for me to be ordained with him,
and so arranged this.

During seminary, I had united with Asylum Hill Congregational Church by transfer of letter, when the girls I had been
teaching entered on confession of faith. My home congregation
(Wesleyan Methodist), having been in touch with me several
times a year during college and seminary, had kept my licensure
active. When I wrote requesting release to another denomination,
along with confirmation of my license, the church recommended
me warmly and without criticizing my decision. The large Hartford Association of Ministers, all men, examined me along with
three male candidates, making it neither more nor less difficult
for me to pass inspection, then licensed me as a first step toward
the Congregational ministry.

When the time arrived for the Association in northern Maine
to examine us for ordination, however, the men (who asked all
the questions, although women were present too as delegates to
the examining council) gave me a much easier time than my

husband, but we were both approved. One woman had a part in the service of ordination, Hilda Ives, a veteran New England minister. She offered the ordaining prayer, laying one hand on my head, the other on my husband's.[2]

My husband had long had the urge to go West, and the second year of our marriage found us in Montana where I was soon asked, train connections being possible, to become the part-time pastor at Custer. Our first son was born during this time, my church and my husband's both predicting that he would become a minister which, in due time, he did.

There is seldom adequate secretarial assistance in small churches and my husband's two, on the Huntley Irrigation Project (Ballantine and Pompeys Pillar), were no exception. We had no church secretary, and I would have been glad to do the work, but he would not hear of it. "You must use your seminary education," he said, "and we will find volunteers for the typewriter."

When we moved to a larger church at Glendive, Montana, I helped with youth work and leadership education in our own congregation, but other denominations, discovering that I was ordained, were soon asking me to speak from their pulpits, when they needed a supply, and to address various groups. Our second son had been born, and so I did not look for a pastorate of my own.

After five years at Glendive, Royal wanted to return to seminary for graduate work. I was sympathetic, but the thought of keeping two lively little boys quiet enough, in a small apartment, for him to study and write a thesis seemed fair neither to him nor to them. Too, even with his fellowship money, it would have been a precarious move financially. Difficult as it might prove, I felt a separation of some months would be preferable, and persuaded both Royal and the seminary to agree to it. Dean Potter said, "I can see that the shoe may not fit now, but you too must come back on a future sabbatical." The church had not accepted my husband's resignation, as they wanted him to return, and at once called me to act as interim pastor. We were able to secure a German girl, Clara Hess, to live with us to keep the

house and care for the children. She loved them and was most
efficient. My husband was able to come home for two vacations
during the year, and we wrote almost every day.

The church in Glendive was larger than a woman would have
been asked to serve ordinarily, but men and women alike were
cooperative, passing over my mistakes with good humor. I in-
nocently presided at the first meeting of the Board of Deacons.
Later, one of the men told me that the senior deacon should
have done that, and I apologized to him, asking why he had not
suggested that I move out of his chair. "I just wanted to see how
you would handle it," he chuckled. If only for contrast, one
ought to provide the relief of a little harsh static here but,
unfortunately, I cannot. His attitude was characteristic of the
congregation.

Preaching

I had not had the responsibility of a weekly sermon for some
time, and trying to open my mind in prayer and preparation
brought memories of my own failures so numerous and nauseous
that I could not hear God. I had yelled at the boys for a trifle.
I had cut short a telephone conversation with a woman who
would have talked an hour, and no doubt needed help. There
were calls on the aging and chronic invalids that I should have
made and had not. "Don't look at me," I said to the Presence,
"your people need bread," and the bread, when it came, was as
much for me as for them.

Several experiences in preaching that year filled me with wonder as to what speaking God's words meant. Once during August,
when I was preaching at union services for three congregations
in the Methodist building, I fought what wanted to be said. The
words from Jeremiah, already so significant in my own life, kept
returning: "Yea, I have loved thee with an everlasting love:
therefore with lovingkindness have I drawn thee." "Summer
laziness," I told myself. "I've preached on that text a number of
times and don't want to work." But these thoughts had not appeared in any other sermon. It was as though they were addressed to persons in the depths of despair, persons who could

not go on believing in the goodness of God. Anyone who knows the church at all knows that the minister speaks only to the saints in August, and to relatively few of them. The sermon depressed me because it was too deep and seemed intended for a desolate people, almost as though the pulpit were going to war with death itself.

Monday morning the phone rang, and a Methodist woman with whom I was well acquainted asked, "Did you know that . . . ?" An engineer of the Northern Pacific Railway, dusting off his hands at the end of a run, had noted blood on the engine and casually remarked, "We must have struck some small animal." The "small animal," it developed, was his son who had been on the trestle as the train roared in. A few years earlier, the family had lost their only daughter through leukemia. The little boy had been their one remaining child. The mother, whom I did not know, was in church that morning, and members of the Methodist congregation, their intimate friends, who had heard of the tragedy, were suffering with them.

It would be easy enough to say that I had picked up some psychic current in preparing the sermon that proved appropriate that morning, but this explanation does not satisfy me if it means some special gift. Rather, I believe, prayer itself, when centered on God and concerned for human beings, brings us into a different dimension in life where much exploration remains to be made.

On another occasion, as I finished writing a sermon and was reading it over, I noticed what seemed an unnatural bulge at one place, and was just ready to strike out a paragraph when I heard, "Let it stay." Later, in preaching, I was moved to expand what I had thought of omitting. At the door, a woman asked to speak with me. As we went into the study, she referred at once to that part of the sermon, and shared a problem on which she thought I might be able to shed some light.

On still another occasion, in reading over a sermon, I felt led to strike out a sentence, but it sounded so fine that I decided not to allow myself to become fanatical, and left it in. The next week, a member of the church inquired what I had meant by it: "I

became so intrigued with that thought that I missed the rest."
There were other similar incidents in the years ahead.

Up to this time, I had felt that, after prayer, study, and every
effort to make adequate preparation for preaching, the sermon
really was the truth of God. I was speaking his words. But now,
a puzzling circumstance made me wonder. Occasionally, someone
would refer to something "you said in your sermon" that I had
never said, nor even thought. Pondering this, I suddenly realized
that there was no locus of authority in the sermon at all. My
words were merely serving as a vehicle to evoke meanings the
Holy Spirit wished to convey. Each mind was busy in the context
of its own experience, quite unrelated to mine, and each person
was hearing in his own language. I began to regard preaching as
sacramental and to see that the minister fails by disobedience.
The requirement is faithfulness; God alone knows truth.

A Changing Life-style

When my husband returned, I was glad to drop back into part-
time work, for I felt the need of a closer relationship with our
children. They were getting good care, but someone else was
talking with them most of the time and answering their questions.
The person doing it was trustworthy; perhaps I was only jealous,
but I was their mother and I wanted to do it myself. So Royal's
return, aside from adjusting to each other again, posed no problem. We were glad to be together again as a family.

The next call was to Morris, Minnesota, and then to Minneapolis. The boys were in school. I was giving every possible
moment to our congregation or to other church groups, with no
paid position, but often receiving honorariums.

Studying the shape my ministry was taking, I wondered
whether a woman can serve more effectively married or single.
I had no qualms about my personal decision. It was easy to
identify with both women and children because I was married
and had children of my own. My husband always referred women
who would need extended counseling to me, feeling that I could
accomplish more with them than he could, or should try to do.
Many men are quick to see that a woman minister may be a

sexual threat when she tries to work closely with men, but have blind spots about the possible sexual involvement their ministries may pose for women. I think team ministries will be the long-term solution for this.

While we lived in Minnesota, there was a steady flow of opportunity to do the work for which seminary had prepared me, but all that changed very suddenly when Royal was called to the Central South as conference minister and felt he should go. The change was welcome to me, too, for several reasons: My husband had the gifts and experience necessary for this new work. He was familiar with rural, small-town, and urban fields. In graduate study, he had made an analysis and study of the historical development of the denomination's work in the state of Montana. He was a good administrator and was interested in helping both ministers and lay persons find and grow in their special abilities. As for myself, the telephone and doorbell in Minneapolis had been making sustained study and prayer almost impossible.

In Oklahoma City, our new home, I was no longer the wife of a local pastor, nor did it seem wise to take up the kind of work in the local churches that I had done previously. There was abundant time for meditation but, after a while, I felt the need to return to action. One morning, reflecting upon the parable of the talents, glad for uninterrupted time to think about anything, it struck me that I was doing no work outside my own home. The churches of our denomination that needed pastoral service were at a distance and public transportation was seldom feasible; as I have said, driving was out of the question for me. Was lack of mobility, created by a family, the result of having chosen marriage *instead of* ministry? I was tempted to think so. The boys were in school, my husband had to travel, and I was the anchor woman. My one talent was buried. Into the midst of these self-accusing thoughts, the Presence spoke, "Let's be specific. What have you been burying, and where?"

As I tried to find concrete answers, I realized that I had been looking hopefully in many directions. There is always busy work for women, but nothing had seemed right. "What is most important to you?" the Presence asked. "What are your central prayers?"

Three emerged: the unity of our family in Christ, the purification and unity of the church, and that every person in the world might know God. "These are big prayers," the Presence replied.

"But are they good prayers?"

"They are good prayers." But there was a premonition of pain.

Time passed, and opportunities presented themselves. I became active in what is now Church Women United. I served for many years on the faculty of the Methodist Summer School of Missions, leading large classes, gathered from various localities of the state, in the study of spiritual life or home missions. I was also receiving many invitations to speak to groups of Methodists and Disciples of Christ. As a result, a small interdenominational group for Bible study and prayer was meeting weekly in our home. I had taken the presidency of the women in our own Congregational Conference as a temporary expedient, to search out leadership in Oklahoma and Texas for education, social action, and mission. As soon as the Woman's Board was functioning well, I withdrew from office.

Both my husband and I have always had confidence in the laity of the church. Beginning with Bible study and prayer, we had urged them to become proficient in areas of their special interests, to read and think about significant books, to attend special conferences with a view to developing Christian leadership in their fields. My husband had noted the near collapse of various local churches after the resignation of "charismatic" (in the popular sense) ministers, and he had always wanted to leave our congregations with an understanding of their mission that would continue after his pastorates were concluded. We were in agreement on this, and the last thing I wanted to do was to encourage dependency.

But with the boys away all day and my husband traveling about half the time, there was not enough to keep me busy in the church. I resolved to look for a job and thought of high school teaching. "No," the boys chorused, "they would slaughter you." Lack of experience in the classroom, it turned out, made a position in the city schools impossible. Nor did my husband take a cheerful view of my full-time employment until I told him that he would have to choose between a working wife and a neurotic one. Checking with a college dean as to the possibility of teaching religion, he asked, "Could you handle Christian education?"

"I don't think so," I said doubtfully. That was the only opening.

"If you are determined to work," my husband remarked, "I can't think why you feel unqualified to teach Christian education at the college level." Going back to the dean, I found that he had just hired a woman who, he said, "does not have your qualifications." As we talked briefly, it seemed to me that the work had been saved for her providentially. I did not think it would have been the right work for me.

Seeing no teaching in sight, I went to the state employment office and took tests. I failed shorthand, and the ancient typewriter broke down during the typing test. I had had high speed in both subjects and, in a fury of frustration, I got everyone who could tolerate me to dictate anything that took his fancy, then read it back. Returning to the state office, I was told, "Usually we don't repeat the tests for six months so people can brush up, but since the typewriter broke down, you may take them again now." This time I passed with flying colors, and they told me they feared the jobs that were open would not pay enough to match my skill. But finally I took a stenographic job in state Child Welfare.

It had not been my intention to publicize the fact that I was a minister, as I felt it would create an unnecessary barrier but, via the grapevine, everyone already knew and was on guard. The girls in the office were cautious but generous in their willingness to help me learn routines. They kept studying my angle, but eventually decided I was one of them.

As I became acquainted with child welfare supervisors and workers, they frequently expressed interest in my professional opinion as a minister and gave me theirs. On one occasion, after dictating a case study on an unwed mother, a supervisor said, "I would like nothing better than to refer this girl to a minister, but her home town is remote, and I do not know the church there. Without knowing, I cannot do it. Some are so lacking in compassion." I could have documented her remark with a few illustrations of my own, as far as churches were concerned, though I knew no minister who would have lacked compassion.

Talking about the problem of promiscuity with a visiting friend who headed up the child welfare work in another state, she said, "When a girl has slept with her father from the time she was ten years old, or with the boys in an inner city neighborhood, what else can we expect? Going to bed with different men every night is no more offensive to her than sitting down to meals at different tables." High moral standards may be found in impoverished families, but they are maintained against monstrous odds in ghetto areas.[3] Many churches are filled with privileged, middle-class persons who have no conception of the agonies of those who try to maintain a good family life but lack their advantages.

The sheer volume of human suffering was almost more than I could bear at times. A long series of letters from the same woman, for example, would have broken up a stone. She was begging for the return of her young son who had been removed from her custody. Sensing my distress, a supervisor said sympathetically, "That woman is the most notorious prostitute in the district, and the boy sees it all. The judge will never give him back." Her realism did not hide the fact that she, too, felt the pain of the situation, but what could be done about it? Who could blame the judge? Nevertheless, the mother, uninvolved emotionally with the men she served, as nearly all prostitutes are, still had a passionate love for her child. A smug person might say, "In that case, let her change her profession." A pious, but callous verdict. What of the social inertia that winks at blighted, crime-producing neighborhoods and allows subhuman conditions to go on decade after decade with degrading effects upon human life? What is the self-appointed judge doing to hasten change in those who have given up hope, but still cling to the remnants of human love?

I worked, also, with case studies on adoptive and foster homes, and became familiar with interstate and international problems in child welfare. So, I began to recognize a fourfold providence in this period of my life: First, I received a free and practical course in the complexities of social work. Second, this job left me free to meet any call for service from the church. My supervisor was fully cooperative. I could go with pay if I had the time coming, without, if I did not, and, for my part, I declined the chance for advancement to a more responsible position where this degree of freedom could not have been given. A third benefit lay in an increasing ability to see the church from an outside, secular point of view where its odd mixture of success and failure is thrown into relief. But the fourth and greatest gain of all came from being where I could witness the most unexpected manifestations of God's love in those who never went to church at all. I kept wondering at the source of their strength, and began to suspect the Presence of wide extracurricular activity. Lay ministry I had long accepted. It was harder to assimilate the fact that authentic ministry also goes on outside the visible church. This does not make the church unnecessary, but shows that it has anonymous allies sharing its love of human beings.

My presuppositions were challenged, my focus of attention was broadening. I was, in fact, learning a whole new language with its own clichés that, strangely, made the clichés of religion a little easier to recognize.

The Presence did not allow me to be comfortable in an office setting too long, however, for I began receiving requests to write —first an article, and then other materials for use in Christian periodicals. After they had been published, I read them over. They sounded so boring that I concluded, if I were going to write, I should learn how. So I took four correspondence courses with the University of Oklahoma.

In the meanwhile, I had been called to preach regularly again in a rural church that had arranged for my transportation, but I was no longer thinking of the ministry in traditional terms alone, and it did not seem to me that any limitation at all should be placed upon functions that might suitably be termed ministries. God is opening up new frontiers, and his word can be heard in peculiar places today.

CHAPTER 5

The People of God—Where?

As I HAVE SAID, WHEN WE MOVED BACK TO THE CITY IN MY early adolescence, my faith began to die. It is not hard to see what happened. I had been shut off from the community of faith. There was no lack of churches, and we returned to the one where we had gone to Sunday school as small children, though it was some distance from our new home. The minister called and, after talking with us, secured a letter transferring my membership. It was the only personal touch I ever had with him. This is not to find fault. The size of many city congregations precludes contact between pastor and parishioners, except on a superficial level, unless they are officers, very active in the church, or passing through a crisis.

Our Sunday school teacher, with whom I spent less than an hour a week, was charming and friendly, but all the rest of the time I was under influences pulling in the opposite direction. Without strong group support, my beginning Christian life drooped, so I prayed, "If you will give me again the desire I had for you before we came back here, I will seek you till I find you if it takes to the last day of my life." The prayer was met by total silence, and it was years before I saw the connection between it and what followed.

A Hidden Answer

My brothers and I had to pass a small frame church on the way to our own, and one night we decided to go in and see what it was like. A revival meeting was in process with a bombastic evangelist who did not appeal to me in the least. But from that night on, my brothers, declaring, "It's better than a circus," refused to pass that church. They had the majority vote (two to one), and felt that they were fully discharging any obligation to my membership by walking the extra distance Sunday morning. After a polite inquiry as to whether or not we belonged to another church, the small congregation did not invite us to become regular attendants, but one woman confided, "Our own pastor is much better than this evangelist. We hope you will have a chance to hear him."

When the revival was over and those who follow such meetings had disappeared, the pastor preached and, immediately, won my absorbed attention. Gradually, over a period of nearly two years, I found in that group what had been slipping away from me. After the dismissal of evening worship, from a dozen to twenty of the members frequently gathered about the altar for prayer. They took up one another's burdens, as suggested by the apostle Paul, and I eventually shared mine, and received help and encouragement. The constant emphasis of this little fellowship was on yielding oneself wholly to God. That is the way to reality.[1] They believed that no one could have authentic knowledge of God apart from such self-giving. So this was the direction of my prayer, but it was wavering. Emotions fluctuated, and my purpose shifted, depending on whether I was with the church or with friends at school. Also, I wanted to be free to think for myself.

One day I asked the minister if he thought it would be all right for me to read books by atheists. He was puzzled. "Why do you want to read them?" he asked.

"I guess I just want to find out what people have to say against God."

He was thoughtful for a moment, then burst out laughing. "The Christian gospel can hold up its head in the light of truth from any quarter," he said. "Read anything you want, only read equally on both sides of the question, and pray; you can trust the Holy Spirit to guide you into truth." It would have been within his power to control my leisure-time reading for a few more years, but he did not choose to do so, even though he may have had some misgivings about where the reading might lead.

Under this man's influence, my longing for God increased and stabilized. One night, in prayer at home, I knew that the Holy Spirit was coming, but remembered the church and asked, "Wait —they have prayed so long; I would like to be with them when you come." There was instant acquiescence.

The following Sunday night saw the inrushing of divine Presence so great that the course of my life was permanently fixed. It was a quiet, intense experience, and the church was one in joy with me. Shortly after this, our pastor resigned to retire, and I prayed fervently, "Let me have his ministry just one more year." Under the strong urging of the congregation, for we were all of the same mind, he decided to remain a while longer. Several biblical sayings will always be incandescent because of sermons he preached that last year. I have forgotten what he said, but can never forget the biblical words his preaching illuminated. One was, "How can ye believe, which receive honour one of another, and seek not the honour that cometh from God only (John 5:44, KJV)?" At the end of the year, I left to continue my schooling. He retired and, soon after, died.

Crisis

During my sophomore year in college, I became aware of a disturbing drift away from God again. This had been going on for some time before I realized that the Presence had not been speaking through the Bible, sermons I heard, personal relationships, or in prayer. I had listened and been led in my own sermon preparation, but this was not quite the same thing. When I tried to pray, there was only silence that went on and on unbroken, while the religious talk at Taylor became more and more irritating. Engrossed in several areas of study, intellectual concerns (as with Bertrand Russell and Simone de Beauvoir) were making preaching and religion in general seem shallow. I ached for the fellowship of prayer in my home church, but there was no way back, and I could not find its equal anywhere I looked—and I did look.

Finally, I closed the door on my past life, including God, and told my roommate, "One cannot develop spiritually and intellectually at the same time, and I am choosing intellectual growth." The inner atmosphere became very cold. Bertrand Russell does not exaggerate the chill of the universe, nor does Jean-Paul Sartre overrate the dreadfulness of freedom. What had been the silence of God became his felt absence. All desire for prayer ceased; the very thought of it was obnoxious. When asked to go with the gospel-teams, my reply was, "I have nothing to say," with no further explanation.

My closest friends among the women were distressed, my roommate saying one Sunday afternoon, "I wish you would just look at your journals." These were not diaries, but books in which I had written several times a month from the time I was fourteen. Following her suggestion, my eyes fell on the words, "If ever I doubt the reality I have known tonight, let me be stabbed back to my senses." It was an account of the time I had prayed, "Let me see your countenance, let me hear your voice." The stab of memory came, quick and powerful, but there was nothing to be done about it. That chapter had come to an end.

"Don't you believe in *anything, anyone?*" my roommate pleaded. After a moment of thought, I answered, "I believe in Mrs. Bair." The girls sent for her, one of them giving up her music tuition for the next semester so they could enclose the money. I did not learn of her sacrifice for many years.

As soon as she received the letter, Mrs. Bair phoned. "The girls tell me you have lost your faith," she said, "but I will never believe it unless I hear it from you."

I burst into tears.

"I'll be there."

When she arrived and I tried to pray, it was as though hands, as strong as the roots of very old trees, were strangling me, but Mrs. Bair held on, with wisdom born of love for God and for me, until a sense of the divine Presence, peace, and forgiveness became real again. But the exuberant joy I had known before did not return. At the time, it seemed to me that such joy is for children, and I had grown up; ordinary human happiness was all anyone ought to expect. Now, however, I think the absence of great joy at that time was due to my inability to forgive myself, a by-product of pride so ingrained as to be unrecognizable. But, at least, the inner emptiness and gloom were gone, and friendship with Dr. Ayres deepened and became a steadying factor. In a generally cheerful state of mind, I finished college, went through seminary, married, had one child, and was expecting another.

Mediocrity

Life was hectic but good. We had baby-sitters and domestic help as needed. I can recall no feeling of imprisonment, but was able to work with my husband in the church about half time. At home, though, the evenings were long. I did not resent his absence because I knew that it was of crucial importance to the church that he meet with committees, call on newcomers when husbands were at home, and speak at various gatherings. I did much speaking and attended many meetings myself.

One evening, however, I faced the fact that I was unspeakably bored with the inane woman's magazine I was reading. Tossing it aside, I remembered that there had been a time when long evenings alone would have been valued as an opportunity for prayer, but there was no impulse toward prayer now. Why? I must be sick—sick enough to die in a spiritual sense.

I picked up a Bible and read here and there, but nothing spoke to me until I noticed that one verse kept falling under my eyes in a most disconcerting way. The binding of the book did not seem to be responsible for the fact that I kept seeing, "Behold, the Lord's hand is not shortened, that it cannot save; nor his ear heavy, that it cannot hear: But your iniquities have separated between you and your God, and your sins have hid his face from you, that he will not hear (Isa. 59:1-2, KJV)." I was conscious of no sins or iniquities. The words irked me by what seemed to be their irrelevance, but still there was a pressure about them. "Are you speaking to me through this prophet?" I asked the Presence.

"If you are telling me that I have sinned, how can that have meaning for me unless I *feel* like a sinner? You love truth. You wouldn't want me fabricating things to confess to you."

There was silent acceptance of what I did not know was a challenge, and gradually, over a period of time, self-knowledge drove me to the brink of despair, where the Presence caught me with the words, "There is no sin so great as despair, because it questions the very goodness of God." I stopped and waited. Mediocrity in anyone who has known the Presence is betrayal, but what is the cure for it? I had not the faintest idea. Gross sins can be forgiven, but how can a person be forgiven for what he *is*? Philip Leon's book, *The Philosophy of Courage*, delivered a special message to me during that period.[2]

Holy Communion

When the next quarterly service of Holy Communion arrived in our church, I went with no particular expectation, but an amazing thing happened. All at once, as my husband read the words instituting the sacrament, it was as though he were completely enveloped by the Presence that was speaking and acting through him. It was the same Presence that had responded to my prayer, "Let me see your face; let me hear your voice," and, once again, I was overwhelmed with adoration, because I became aware of Christ, offering his life for us and *to us*. Everything that I had known as a girl in my early teens was given back, and much more.[3] Gratitude welled up for what I thought was some kind of special blessing. I did not guess that Holy Communion would never again be the same for me. So penetrating was the consciousness of the divine Presence that it became necessary to pray, in coming years, that all emotion be removed at the reception of this sacrament. This prayer was answered, and there was nothing but the naked reality of communion itself where the words sometimes heard inwardly were piercingly clear and, seemingly, on a number of occasions, prophetic.

But I did not know what to do about it. A minister must preach and celebrate the sacrament. What was my responsibility in interpreting it to the laity? Trying to find out through reading and study, I recall that the writings of Brilioth, discovered while we lived in Minneapolis, were illuminating.[4] A trivial incident at a social gathering of Twin City ministers of our denomination and their wives also affected me. Someone noted a crucifix in the living room and asked why it was turned the wrong way. The host, who had been a chaplain in the armed services, jokingly said that he had turned his altar cross around, showing the crucifix on the other side, to see if it would be noticed. "Each is only half a symbol," I thought. "You have to have the crucifix and the empty cross together to mean anything. What are crucifixion and resurrection (symbolized by the empty cross) when seen apart?"

It was about this time that we moved to Oklahoma City, and ministers were beginning to carry small crosses in their wallets as a reminder of stewardship in the midst of our American affluence. I was still wrestling with theological problems relative to the sacrament, and the faultiness of half a symbol had remained with me. I decided I wanted a tiny crucifix to carry in my purse too. So I went to the Catholic Bookstore to look for one. A friend went along and was glancing at items in the pamphlet rack while I shopped. When I rejoined her, I saw a few booklets I wanted to read and picked up another, putting it down hurriedly because both title and cover were repulsive, but the Presence said, "The answers to your questions are in that book." It was beyond belief, but I purchased it with two others and did not open it until I had read them first. To my astonishment, great enlightenment came from the first part of the book, but the last had no meaning whatever for me. After pondering the helpful sections for about six months, I wrote to the author, a Benedictine monk. In replying, he advised me to go to a Catholic church and take instructions. Appalled and indignant, I wrote him that I felt no attraction whatever toward Catholicism. Our correspondence continued, but, when we met later, there was no talk of conversion; we remained good friends until his death.

Two attitudes were evolving side by side in my mind. First, an increasing desire for the unity of all Christians and, second, a felt need for Holy Communion because this seemed to bring a much greater clarity to my prayer life. The Council of Churches, as well as the Oklahoma City prayer groups that met together from time to time, were a centripetal force, as it seemed to me, of the Holy Spirit. The fact that the Lord's Supper was observed only four times a year in my own church[5] led me to attend mid-week Episcopal worship at times, and I came to love their liturgy. But the cleft between Catholicism and Protestantism was complete at the grass-roots level then, and I felt impelled to try to bridge it. Studying Catholic theology and seeking contacts of some depth with Catholic people made me realize that we were all poorer for our divisions. I felt a constant, strong, inner pressure to pray for unity.

Going to my own church in this frame of mind one Communion Sunday, I could not believe my ears when the minister paused following the words of institution to expound all that they did not mean.[6] "I cannot stand any more of this," I said to our Lord. "Roman Catholics at least know that the Presence in this sacrament is real. I belong with them. I am going to become a Roman Catholic."

The reply was, "You must not do this without a sign from me."

Dismayed and aware from earlier experience that a sign (which should not be sought) would be both unpredictable and unmistakable, I felt as though the words were shutting me out of the church entirely. But the Holy Spirit quickly brought me into a large place; the walls of denominationalism had collapsed, and the church in which I stood, the foundation of God, needed no adjectives to describe it. I saw that human words could never permanently contradict that one word, heard through the centuries; what our Lord intended his followers to be, they would, in his time, become. Ever since that morning I have believed that it is the word of God that validates the sacrament; the minister or priest is only a vehicle.

A Widening Ministry

I had been preparing to write, and now felt that I wanted to interpret Protestant attitudes for Catholics, and Catholic attitudes for Protestants. I was as close to one part of the church as to the others. My first articles, submitted to Catholic periodicals, were accepted. One had gone to a popular weekly, the other to a scholarly journal.[7] I continued to write about equally for Catholics and Protestants. Then dialogue groups came on the scene and, when we moved East, I became active in them.

But the climate is still changing. In writing for Catholic and Protestant magazines now, one is accepted as a Christian. Some few periodicals open their pages to dialogue with those of other religions or no religion. The church, for all its divisions, is moving into greater communication with the world.

In 1960, I went back to seminary for the sabbatical Dr. Potter had said I must take when the time was right. David, our younger son, and Fonda had married, and they moved into our home while I was away so that Royal, when he traveled, did not have to return to an empty house. Our older son, Bricker, had also married and was in seminary, so I often spent weekends with him and Carolyn. I had planned all my studies and seminars with a view to increasing mutual understanding between Catholics and Protestants. During this period, a woman from Pakistan asked me, "Why should Christians not bury their identity in a Muslim community, and simply live the love of God and man as we have been told to do?" Maintenance of identity seemed crucial to me, but what identity is it that we must keep?

Certainly denominational identity is important to fewer and fewer people today, but is there not an identity in Christ that can be kept without secondary labels? If we believe in the real Presence in the eucharist,[8] and do not insist upon theological precisions beyond what each worshiper can grasp for himself, will not Christ lead us all into a deepening relationship with God, one another, and the world? Apart from such a witness to our unity as the Lord's Supper itself is, what of significance have we to say to the world torn by disunity? We talk instead among ourselves, each church assuming an individual, ambiguous right to speak the word of the Lord with authority. It seems to me that we are on the threshold of death to sectarianism and of such rebirth of the church as will make our old divisions as incredible to ourselves as they have long been to that part of the world that refuses to take us seriously because of them.

The individual Christian has a part, a mission, in this, and no one save the divine Presence can tell him what it is. The path into awareness of that Presence is the intention to put ourselves unconditionally into his hands, irrespective of fluctuating emotions, with every power of thought, and with trust in his strategy. This does not mean "consensus." Our backgrounds are too different to entertain any such hope yet. Our present experiences are too diverse. The common theological ground is apparently still insufficient,[9] but there is one Lord who is able to lead us on toward the kind of unity that can become a paradigm for mankind. We shall have to be content with mutual love about one table, where the visible human host knows that his function is strictly representative and not determinative, until we can see where our varying missions are going to converge. To repeat my earlier question: Whose word is it that makes the visible sacrament Holy Communion—God's or man's? Will not those who think it is God's show their faith in the real Presence by fearlessly joining others who are responding to the invitation of the living Christ? True, there are many shades of belief and degrees of maturity of faith, but is an unbeliever likely to be attracted to such a celebration as the eucharist and, if he is, can we rule out the possibility that he, too, may be receiving an invitation from the true host, the Lord of love himself?

Theologians, of course, will see a pitfall here, the danger of which I may seem unaware, covered as it is by the branches and dead leaves of yesterday. Is the real Presence merely subjective, or is there objective reality in this sacrament? Or to put it another way, is God only in man, or is he transcendent? In an agony of intellectual distress, I once inquired of the Presence, when he was speaking to me: "Do these words come from you, or from my own deep self?"

"What difference does it make?" he asked. (The Presence, I have discovered, likes questions related to action rather than speculation.)

"If they come from ourselves," I replied, "we don't feel we can trust them all the way. If they come from you, we can."

"What difference does it make," he repeated, "if the words lead you toward the truth?" Is there not an inner witness to this leading? But human beings have an inveterate wish for truth in packaged form.

Freedom and Joy

In one form or another, the question persisted. The drift from God comes about so easily, so unconsciously. At the time my early joy was restored in Holy Communion, I longed so much for some permanent assurance that I would never be alone again, and for days I kept hearing the words "The Father himself loves you (John 16:27)." I thought I must be going to preach on that subject, but no sermon came, and eventually it dawned on me that the biblical word was personal once again.

Later, when the footing seemed precarious, I begged God to take away my freedom. "I will leave you again," I predicted, "because that is the way I am." I felt that I could not bear another separation. Praying the same prayer day after day was fruitless, answered only by silence. Then, finally, the Presence said, "I cannot take your freedom without taking your joy, and I am unwilling to do that."

Reflecting, I asked, "But you will guarantee my faith?"

"I can never guarantee your faith," was the reply, "only the ground of your faith."

This was not enough security. I was afraid of myself. Then he asked, "Is it so hard to keep looking at one you already love? The only failure would be in forgetting to look. Look and look until you can never look away."

Suddenly I realized that it had been years since loving God had been an effort. He is lovable and himself evokes love if we look steadfastly in his direction. The fear melted for the time.

But a few days later, I wakened with clouded thoughts and complained, "That veil is there again."

"It is made of nothing more substantial than your own thoughts," the Presence said. "Push them aside and come."

So, no matter what the external circumstances, when we search, faith is evoked, generation after generation, by the one whose love brought us into being. The people of God, whoever and wherever they are, live to bear witness to that love. Moreover, they have a world view of their own, centered upon the living God and his purpose with the human race.

PART III

Death or Life

CHAPTER 6

Coping with Death

WHATEVER OUR WORLD VIEW, IF LIFE IS TO HAVE ULTIMATE meaning for the individual, that meaning must be perceived through eyes other than those in our faces for, as anyone can plainly see, observable life ends in death. And yet, there are vast numbers of people, even in this age of science and technology, who believe that life is something else, that, homelike as our bodies become, when they have served their purpose, we move on. To *what*, and *what* moves on? Do the superhighways of existence have more exits than the one to death? If they do, what travel bureau or scouting expedition issues the information? Is not Christian faith merely a sedative for those who find the pain of reality too sharp? In the last chapter, we shall explore the views reached by Bertrand Russell, Simone de Beauvoir, Eugenia Price, and myself.

But in the meanwhile, there is the undisputed fact that society must face: apart from all lofty thought, physical death is the unavoidable outcome for everyone. The culture is permeated by unsolved problems with regard to it that bring the various professions into dialogue among themselves and with the public in general. Christians must face these difficult questions, too, and try to struggle through, with the rest of mankind, to temporary solutions.

The medical profession faces challenges on certain of its basic assumptions. State legislatures are under pressure to update laws relating to death. The church has been developing special ministries for the aging. The behavioral sciences sense their responsibility for the dying person; he is no longer within the province of physician and clergyman alone. The most hopeful sign, though, is professional collaboration; no discipline can do its best work alone.

Industrial development and public health policies continue to push life expectancy upward. In the Middle Ages, people could anticipate living into their thirties; today it is not unusual for a person to live into his seventies, eighties, or even nineties. Recently a man aged 104 told a friend he could not understand why his doctor seemed unable to prescribe medicine that would give him "a little pep." It has been predicted that the life span can be stretched to 150 years in the light of knowledge now in hand. Anyone who visits persons in their nineties will know how typical a remark, made to me, is: "I hope I get off the earth before that time comes." An extension of time is not necessarily good news. How many look forward to the operations involved in the installation of donated organs? It seems quite obvious that organic frames are not destined to permanency and, if they could be made so, would not the number of suicides increase out of sheer boredom?

Medicine

In medical school, the prospective physician must make up his mind whether he will specialize, go into general practice, or enter a research program. It is a tough decision that will affect his whole future attitude toward human beings. When he begins general or special practice, he will become well acquainted with his patients, see them as persons, and act accordingly. If he enters research work, his attention will be focused on the problems he is trying to solve. This does not, to be sure, make him inhumane but, of necessity, he takes a highly objective view of individuals. They are related to the questions on which he is working and not vice versa, as is the case with the doctor on the outside of experimental research. An important element in his decisions is bound to be the future benefit of mankind.

As might be expected, the World Medical Association has had to establish guidelines for clinical research. In 1964, it clearly stated that the nature, purpose, and risk of nontherapeutic research must be clarified for the subject by the physician.[1] That would seem simple enough but, in application, it is not. Parents giving consent for experimentation on children, for example, may have a grossly inadequate grasp of what that consent may involve. Moreover, how can you draw a definite line between therapeutic and nontherapeutic research? For example, in work on the brain it is not possible to give volunteers the ramifications of what may be expected; the research doctor himself does not always know.[2] The further question is being raised: How "voluntary" is the consent of prisoners and mental patients when search for scientific knowledge is unbridled by ethical concerns?[3] Supposing the physical hazards can be predicted, how are psychological effects on particular individuals to be estimated?

These surface inquiries lead into deeper speculations: When a person commits himself to a hospital, to whom does he belong —the medical team, his anxious family, or still to himself? After a sufficient amount of medication has been given, how far is he capable of making life and death decisions about himself? If there is a crisis and his ability is doubtful, then everyone concerned faces the dilemma: does this person, if heroic measures become necessary, want to live or to be permitted to die?

The medical profession has acted upon the assumption that he wants to live, whatever his age; it is, therefore, incumbent upon the doctor and the entire hospital staff to work toward that end. Dr. William A. Nolen, author of *The Making of a Surgeon*, puts it this way in a news article:

> No matter how bad life is, I have yet to find anyone who wants to hurry his departure. . . . If I'm ill I certainly don't want a doctor taking care of me who looks upon death as a big buddy. I want some guy who will fight with every weapon he has to keep me alive, who will struggle against death as long as there's any reasonable chance to win the battle, who will out-fox death if it can possibly be done.

But there are other points of view. A nurse told me of an incident that took place thirty years ago and involved a friend of hers in the same profession. A patient constantly begged to die, moaning, "It's my life. Won't someone help me out of my misery?" The nurse gave the overdose of a drug that brought release. "It was the best thing I ever did," she confided to the woman I interviewed. Such a procedure would be virtually impossible in today's hospital situation.

But nurses are ambivalent. One writes of a patient sixty-eight years old whom she tended in intensive care and greatly admired. A pacemaker saved his life. Two months later, he had to have major abdominal surgery; later, it was necessary to attach a colostomy bag. His heart stopped, but air was forced into his lungs by a resuscitator bag; there was intravenous medication, intracardial stimulation, electrode-connected shock to restart the heart. He moaned, grimaced, and mumbled incoherently. A few weeks later, he had to face an emergency tracheotomy to keep breathing. This patient had lived alone, but, twice a month, an aging sister, whose husband was also ill, made a two-hour bus trip each way for a one-hour visit during which she wept and asked the nurse, "Why do they keep him? Why don't they let him die?"[4]

Beneath her calm professional manner, the nurse was asking the same question, but, at the same time, she was reading Camus' *Notebooks 1935-1942* during her lunch hour. There was an entry characterizing an invalid with both legs amputated and paralyzed all down one side. He says:

They help me when I want to relieve myself. They wash me. I'm practically deaf. But I would never do a thing to cut short a life in which I believe so strongly. I would accept much worse: blindness, deprivation of all my senses, loss of the power of speech and of any contact with the external world—as long as I could feel within me this dark, burning flame which is me and me alive. And I should still give thanks to life for having let me continue to burn with its flame.[5]

The nurse wished she could have heard such words from her patient. It would have been easier. Did he feel this way too? She had no answer.

Who can say what the dying person really wants? Nevertheless, many members of the medical profession are being made fully aware today that there are lengths to which neither patients nor their families want them to go. There comes a time (with old people especially, though it may happen with anyone) when the person, detaching himself from life, is reconciled to going and does not want to be detained.[6] An increasing number of doctors are now open to passive euthanasia, that is, to the withdrawing of artificial supports to life when it cannot be sustained otherwise, and when family members agree that the time for release has come. But here the physician must proceed with caution and be alert to the law, or he may run into trouble.

Law

The root of the legal problem is that we have no standard definition for death. A generation ago the question seemed simple. When the heart stopped beating and the lungs ceased functioning, the person was dead, but today these organs can be kept going by machine. The suggestion has been made by investigators in the fields of ethics and sociology that human vegetables who recognize no one, are unable to speak, move, eat, or keep clean on their own, and who show no possibility of improvement are really dead. Heart and lung action alone do not define life.[7] Some states have already added a third sign of death—the absence of spontaneous brain function.[8] Walter W. Sackett, Jr., a Florida physician, has been wrestling since 1968 for "the right to die with dignity," and Dr. Orlando Lopez brought the case of a seventy-two-year-old Cuban exile who preferred death to very painful treatments, on which Florida Circuit Court Judge David Pepper ruled that "a patient has the right not to be tortured," even if failure to treat means sure death.[9]

We still do not know when a human being is a living person. This affects life at its beginning in problems relating to abortion and at its conclusion in trying to ascertain when specifically human life has ceased.

We come now to the discussion of euthanasia which may be considered under three headings: (1) passive euthanasia, where, as we have said, recovery being impossible, supports to life are withdrawn and nature is allowed to take its course; (2) voluntary euthanasia, where the patient himself has asked to be allowed to die in peace; and (3) active euthanasia, often called "mercy killing," where a sympathizing person terminates the life of another as, for example, by a lethal dose of a drug.

1. There is considerable openness to passive euthanasia now. Where the family requests or concurs, some doctors admit to practicing it; more than a third of the nurses I interviewed favored it. The situation is fluid, and public opinion is changing rapidly. A group of senior citizens at Pilgrim Place in Claremont, California, nearly all of whom have given their lives to Christian work, petitioned the State Bar to start hearings on the advisability of legislation that would protect physicians from civil suit or criminal prosecution if they fail to use surgical, medical, or mechanical devices to prolong life in the terminally ill. The petitioning group was advised the matter could not be handled by the State Bar group as such; interested legislators would have to be enlisted to make the first moves. Public opinion, supporting such legislation, is growing.

2. With regard to voluntary euthanasia, *A Living Will* has been prepared by the Euthanasia Education Fund[10] in which the signer addresses a request to his family, physician, clergyman, and lawyer in case he lives beyond the ability to share in decisions for his future, and is to the effect that he be spared artificial means and heroic measures to prolong his life. *A Living Will* states that the signer fears the "indignity of deterioration, dependence and hopeless pain" more than he fears death and asks that drugs be administered for terminal suffering, even if they hasten the moment of death. While this document is not legally binding, even when properly witnessed, it carries moral weight by indicating that the individual signing it accepts responsibility for

terminating his own life, along with those whose assistance he requests.

Medical doctors often take the position that life on this earth is the highest good known to man and no one has the right to take the initiative in ending it. Dr. Henry A. Davidson says, "As a scientist I conclude that logic is all on the side of euthanasia. As a physician I will not take the power to put someone to death."[11] Walter C. Alvarez, a Chicago physician, who has given much thought to euthanasia, has reached this conclusion:

> I think mainly of two things: (1) not struggling desperately to keep alive an idiot, or a person with an incurable disease, or a person dying in great pain, or a person in great suffering who begs to be left alone; and (2) wishing that we Americans would grant to incurables and great sufferers the right to take an overdose of a drug. I do not want some religious belief to make me horribly cruel.[12]

If this is regarded as sanctioning suicide, psychologist Eustace Chesser says that he would put suicide for rational motives in a wholly different category from pathological suicide, and he questions our right to sentence old people to life when they wish to die.[13] There are many shades of opinion regarding voluntary euthanasia, but those most opposed to it seem to be thinking that the patient cannot tell in advance how he will feel when face to face with death; it is, therefore, wrong to act upon a statement that he has made some years earlier.

3. Whenever a periodical has the courage to publish a first-person article that tries to make a case for active euthanasia (mercy killing), public reaction is charged with emotion and, if one can trust reader response, about equally divided. Accusations of selfishness fly in both directions and those with conflicting points of view assert that they are motivated by love. Some Christians, arguing that there must be a divine purpose behind the existing situation, debate humanists who quake at the thought of a human being forced to live a subhuman life. Others insist

that it brings out the best in us to take care of them, but is it not immoral to prolong useless anguish on such a basis?

And what of those so severely retarded they cannot live in any society, so totally deranged there are never lucid moments, or in the last stage of senility? The general public complains about taxes but, aside from that, shows little concern. The nurse who read Camus and reflected upon the sufferings of her own patient made a suggestion that may be relevant:

> It would seem possible, in this age of world tribunals, that in every hospital there could be a panel of decision that included a doctor, a lawyer, a minister, a nurse, and a member of the patient's family. Certainly there should be some recourse against the senseless continuing of life beyond all hope of recovery.[14]

The average individual would not give fifteen minutes in an effort to imagine what animal or vegetable existence must be for a human. But any suggestion that an interdisciplinary panel examine each case and study his record to find out whether or not conscious life, or the desire for it, remains and, if not, to administer merciful release would fill them with horror that Nazi concentration camp techniques were being proposed here. That there is a root difference between the dispatching of those who have every reason to live and contribute to society and those who can never live on the human level, they cannot fathom. So the cruelty goes on, often under the guise of religious motivation. The commandment "Thou shall not kill," traditionally honored by both Jews and Christians, is solemnly quoted. But the mandates to love God and man have priority, do they not? When sentience in the body of a man, woman, or child is no longer human, would love decree animal or vegetable existence? Would anyone be willing to contemplate such a finale for his own life on earth?

That the ethical problems are complex and may take time to work out can scarcely be denied. For one thing, the individuals who would be the subjects of active euthanasia are beyond communication with others and cannot speak for themselves. But most of us manage to use our imagination where animals are concerned and consider it immoral to allow them to suffer interminably, though we may look the other way when it comes to animals used in medical research. Should it not be possible, if we really cared, to reach humane decisions regarding hopeless human suffering? We no longer hold the opinion that God has condemned women to the full measure of pain nature would allow in childbirth. Babies are helped into the world. Why can we not use our intelligence to cope with life's ending? Must people die by inches? Why do we still blame God for our unmerciful dealings with those from whom *human* life has departed or in whom it has perhaps never existed? Legal solutions, however, must wait for the development of public opinion for which Christians must take their full share of responsibility.

The Behavioral Sciences

When, in the fall of 1965, Dr. Elisabeth Kubler-Ross was asked by four theological students to guide their research on the crisis of death, she found the request intriguing and anticipated little difficulty in granting it. The terminally ill themselves would be the teachers, insofar as they were able and willing, she thought, and both she and the students would learn from them. But the project, reported in her book *On Death and Dying*, proved difficult as well as rewarding. There was no problem with the patients; they were eager for someone to listen to them, but hospital personnel, and especially doctors, were defensive at first, though later they saw the value of the study.[15]

Behavioral scientists expect their disciplines to have an expanding role in care for the critically ill and the dying. The doctor's focus, in their view, is upon the body, and the clergyman's helpfulness is curtailed by the waning of traditional Christian beliefs. Psychiatrist K. R. Eissler says that any help the representative of religion can give comes to a quick end when man has lost his faith in God. People do not become "more pliable to the improbable" in their last hours.[16] Sociologists have a similar attitude, Kurt W. Back stating, "The scientist, and particularly the social scientist, has succeeded the priest as the guide to personal change and . . . to spiritual search. . . . Terms such as guilt, depravity and salvation are avoided; instead we have illness, neurosis and therapy."[17] Writing in *Newsweek*, Arthur Cooper observes that psychiatry has become the religion of the twentieth century, with psychiatrists and psychoanalysts as its high priests.[18] The clergyman, knowing how full his own days are, will naturally think these judgments a bit premature, but at least they indicate that the clergy are no longer alone in trying to meet the mental and emotional problems of patients.

What is it that the psychiatrist thinks he does better than the minister in the care of the dying person? Let us go back a little. Years ago, the personal faith of the sufferer made scant difference in his felt need for the presence of the priest or minister as he neared death. (There were, of course, exceptions.) If he was a believer, the pastor would bolster and inspire his faith. If he was an unbeliever, it could be safely assumed that he was anxious by now about his soul. While the church has never encouraged the postponement of conversion to one's dying hours, it has always believed, in view of Jesus' words to the thief on the cross, "Today you will be with me in Paradise," that one can turn to God and be forgiven even at the last moment. The strong religious coloring of the culture, therefore, made the presence of the clergy appropriate at the approach of death.

But the cultural drift, as we have seen, is toward science and technology now, and doubtless psychiatry is right in the belief that its practitioners can be more relevant than those of the church where religious faith has been nonexistent in the life of one now dying. The psychiatrist will try to identify with the patient in his extreme need in a manner supportive of mental health. His support must be genuine, not counterfeit; falsity will be detected. If the patient has faith, he undergirds it. If unbelief in a future life is present, he accepts it. But how can he be genuine and sincerely identify with such contradictory points of view?

In answering this question, Dr. Eissler calls in the unconscious where, he believes, "the archaic belief in the immortality of the soul" still lies dormant in everyone.[19] Freud had taught that there is no representation of one's own death in the unconscious, a fact that necessitates the conclusion that nothing instinctual inclines one toward belief in his own death.[20] The psychiatrist, in the presence of faith, then, reactivates his own deep, unconscious tendency toward hope. If, on the other hand, the patient has integrated death into his whole mental attitude, the psychiatrist can simply share his sorrow and sympathy concerning the approaching end. He supports the patient's personal integrity in facing life and death. When the psychiatrist finds a capability for growth right to the last as, for example, a greater willingness to forgive enemies, he accompanies the dying person in that "maximum individualization of which he is capable."[21]

It should be noted that no essential antagonism exists between psychiatry and religion. Some psychiatrists, viewing their profession as a Christian calling, have been educated both in the field of their science and in theology, and some clergy, likewise, have the training to employ techniques of psychiatry.[22] There is no reason why the clergy and psychiatrists cannot work together, and often they do.

Sociologists, too, are concerned with the aging and dying.[23] Death usually takes place now in the setting of a larger and more complex institution than the home. Where the patient once felt surrounded by love, sustained by members of his family, he may now feel isolated, abandoned to impersonal medical procedures, while relatives stand helplessly by or fail to appear at all because there is nothing they can do.

Behavioral scientists sometimes criticize persons in medical work for aloofness when there is no chance of a patient's recovery, so that the dying are left to feel forsaken, alone. I asked nurses whether or not they felt such accusations were ever justified. Nearly all were emphatic in their denial, one saying she would not leave a dog to die alone, to say nothing of a human being. Two admitted the criticism might apply to very busy doctors. Two others said a patient might feel abandoned, not knowing how many times the nurses' eyes were on him as they passed the room or slipped in quietly. One said that an individual might be removed from a ward shortly before death and deduce he was being forsaken, whereas he would really be under close observation.

But there was a slight (and understandable) impression of defensiveness. The nurses were aware of the awesomeness of death and the desperate longing for human caring, constantly at hand, that those approaching it experience, a longing that nurses could not possibly meet with all the responsibility they carry. Far more help is needed than they can provide, yet families are so situated that they cannot give the loving terminal care that was possible a generation or two ago. Obviously a new and different way of coping with death is needed. If better plans are to be made, public opinion must be activated.

Religion

The clergy, like other professionals, have been developing specializations, including care for the sick and dying but, because it is hard to be thoroughly objective about performance in one's own discipline, I have asked nurses to give me their candid opinions as to whether or not the clergy can make a vital contribution to the patient when illness is critical or death is coming. Only two nurses felt that ministers, priests, and rabbis can do nothing for the terminally ill. Five felt that their presence was important if requested, but added that the unchurched seldom want to see members of the clergy. One young nurse mentioned that the chaplains in her hospital routinely call on all who are admitted and offer their services if the patient wishes to see them. She felt that when the ice is broken in this way, even unchurched persons may ask for a call if something is bothering them. Doctors and nurses often seem in a hurry, and patients are glad to talk with any professional person who will listen.

The majority of nurses, however, said that whether the clergy can help or not depends entirely upon the individual. Anyone who has a warm, loving relationship with the patient can do much for him in his last conscious hours. If such a relationship exists between patient and pastor, no one can do more. If the minister is merely making a perfunctory call in the name of the church, though, his presence means little or nothing. It may even be threatening, leading the patient to suspect the worst about his condition and lose whatever hope he has. Most nurses felt that the professional training of hospital chaplains makes them more helpful than the regular pastor, unless the latter has had a good prior relationship to the patient.

Psychiatrist Elisabeth Kubler-Ross has given a brief glimpse of her reaction to clergy as she went about her hospital tasks. She found the chaplain an ally, and rabbis, priests, and ministers much less defensive about their work than hospital medical personnel. She was amazed, however, at the number of clergy who felt quite comfortable using a prayer book, or a chapter from the Bible, as the sole communication between themselves and the patients, thus avoiding listening to their needs and being exposed to questions that they (the clergy) might be unable or unwilling to answer.[24] She thus agreed with nurses' comments about a perfunctory ministry. Carl G. Carlozzi, an Episcopal priest, has given a brief but penetrating analysis of the "ecclesiastical defense syndrome" that lies at the root of the perfunctory manner. The priest retires behind the "shield" of his ordination into ritualized action, special language, special attire, or his "very busy life" to elude relationships of depth, substituting a "quick priestly blessing."[25]

I have noted, as did one of the nurses, that questions will surface with the very ill, even if they are not well acquainted with a minister, when he takes time to sit down with them for a little while in a quiet, relaxed manner. For example, one young man, dying in his early forties, sent word that there was a matter he wished to discuss with me. I anticipated some problem related to his own affairs, but it was not that at all. His faith was quivering over the thought of a God who cares only for the future of Christians and would abandon all others. As I talked with him about the divine compassion for each creature, relief and peace came over his face. He was a sensitive and unusually mature person; the Christian's God, as represented to him earlier in life, had been too small to invite his confidence.

It hardly needs to be said that ministers are no less human than those in any other profession. One chaplain will never forget what a patient told him early in his training, "Don't tell me how much God loves me, tell me how much you love me. Then I'll make up my mind about God."[26] The ideal is professional cooperation in the care of the dying.

The Interdisciplinary Approach

The interdisciplinary method is embodied in the very person of Cicely Saunders of England who, first as nurse, then as social worker, and finally as physician, heard the call of Jesus to share his work of healing and comforting. She became the founder and is now medical director of St. Christopher's Hospice near London, which is serving as a model for many in different parts of the world who share her interests.

The idea of a hospice originated in the Middle Ages and referred first to a way station for pilgrims as they traveled across Europe. In France, the term came to apply to homes for the elderly, the incurable, or foundlings. Less than a century ago, a hospice in Dublin was dedicated by the Irish Sisters of Charity to the care of the dying and those who faced prolonged illness. In addition to these traditions, St. Christopher's has drawn upon the practice of medieval hospitals that took in the sick poor who would have dropped in the streets from cold and malnutrition. "All the groups we have mentioned," Dr. Saunders says,

> are gathered within our walls; the elderly residents in the Draper's Wing, the Playgroup members, not foundlings but the children of staff who come and cheer us all by their noisy play, those who need longer term nursing than can be carried out in an ordinary hospital, and who make their home with us and give us all so much in friendship and life, and the very ill to whom we can give a great deal of treatment, often unexpected remission or even cure, but always, we hope, something of real comfort.[27]

Thus, the ages in St. Christopher's family vary from eighteen months to ninety-five years.

Dr. Saunders says that St. Christopher's Hospice was first

thought about in 1948 when a young Pole died in a busy fifty-bed hospital ward and left her five hundred pounds to be "a window in your Home," remarking, "I only want what is in your mind and in your heart." She was a social worker at the time, but the idea grew, plans were made, money raised, and in July 1967 the hospice was opened. Respect and attention to the distressed patient comes first, not alone for his body but for his total person. Listening, compassionate understanding, "just being there," are prime duties of every member of the staff and every worker. Facilities and services have increased steadily.

A research program, making an intensive study of the use of drugs—their pain-relieving qualities, long-term and side effects—is in process. There is a teaching program, too, that draws students from the helping professions for short or long periods. In 1971-72, there were a hundred such residents—doctors, nurses, social workers, and theological students. The hospice provides outpatient service, physiotherapy and occupational therapy, and has a large body of volunteers assisting in many aspects of the work.

In assessing their experience at St. Christopher's, students say they have been impressed by the acceptance of death when it comes, reconciliation to it with no sense of defeatism or forced neglect by doctors, absence of that stratification that puts medical personnel at the top, then staff, and patients and visitors last, the atmosphere of freedom from pain and depression, the liveliness and peacefulness that must be seen to be appreciated. A Christian institution, St. Christopher's also welcomes those of other faiths or no faith at all to both staff and care.

In an address to their Annual General Meeting in 1965, Dr. Saunders said she felt the needs of the dying were summed up in Jesus' words in the Garden of Gethsemane, "Watch with me." Recalling Pope John's remark, "My bags are packed, and I can leave with a tranquil heart at any moment," she prays that St. Christopher's may be able to help people—whether terminal patients or not—to pack their bags with the things *they* need, the things that matter, such as reconciliation, fulfillment, and meaning.[28]

Yale University has been interested in this project for some time and, in 1969, awarded Dr. Saunders an honorary degree in science, recognizing that she has "combined the learning of science and the insight of religion to relieve physical pain and mental anguish" and that she has "advanced the awareness of the humanistic aspects of patient care in all stages of illness." Perhaps an even higher compliment lies in the fact that New Haven, Connecticut, is now well on the way to having a hospice of its own, with task forces working on patient-care, community relations, professional relations, building and site, finance, and research. Hospice, Inc., will be well integrated with existing facilities in the community. A strong program for work with members of the patients' families is contemplated. Staff will include many disciplines: medicine, pharmacology, clergy, nursing, social work, and psychiatry, as well as nonprofessionals. "Having seen how team work is an actuality, not simply a concept, in the Hospice community in England," their Statement says, "we believe we can develop exciting interdisciplinary relationships, health care worker-lay person relationships, shared roles, and relationships across age lines."[29] Much of the philosophy of St. Christopher's has been incorporated in the New Haven plan. The Home Care Program and official Capital Fund drive were initiated in 1973.

There is no consensus among Christians as to how God's kingdom will come, but we are unanimous in praying for its coming and for the doing of God's will on earth. Does not such a prayer imply that we will focus our efforts toward that kingdom, whether we believe it will be inaugurated by human effort or by divine intervention? The setting for the last hours of every person will be conditioned by society's manner of coping with death: as members of society we are involved in the conditioning process. Once we are thoroughly convinced that there can be no such person as a Christian without a Christian vocation that can be ascertained in communion with God, whatever his means of livelihood, we will move out toward many frontiers for the improvement of life on earth. As Thomas Kelly once said, "We cannot die on every cross," but a Christian world view, based upon presuppositions received from Jesus, will send some of us to the aid of the aging and dying.

It is time now to leave the social scene and return, in the next chapter, to a personal consideration of death.

CHAPTER 7

Exit to Death—or Life

THAT EXPERIENCE TEACHES WAS A PSYCHOLOGICAL INSIGHT OF the Roman historian Tacitus, who was born soon after the death of Christ. But what does it teach? Clearly, it does not lead mankind to a universally accepted knowledge. Different presuppositions, the wide assortment of objects that capture and hold our attention, our ability to change, the talk and writing to which we respond, all affect what life can teach us. We devote ourselves to what we most want to know.

We may come to faith in God, or we may rule God out, concluding that any possible hope rests with man. Probably few of us have completely consistent world views. One may have a relatively pagan outlook on life into which he has stirred some religious observances with the thought that God is a last resort, "just in case." Another may have a Christian slant in general but refuse to face and do anything about actions that imply spots of atheism. So we approach old age, if we are fortunate enough to live this long, in an inner world fashioned by our unique experience. Simone de Beauvoir saw this clearly when she said that, knowingly or unknowingly, we prepare a given old age for ourselves by our way of life. The superhighways of existence run side by side but, barring accidents, we are all along maneuvering toward the lane by which we shall leave this world, not in any physical sense, of course, for no one can foresee the time and manner of his departure, but in a mental and spiritual sense.

As we admitted in the beginning, what lies beyond the exits

is known only to God. Great religious teachers have shared their views, in persuasive ways, as coming from God. Christians believe that tidings were received from beyond the grave, that there was a "resurrection," confirming the victory of one who loved God and man perfectly, and calls us to trust and follow him. But there is no scientific evidence of this that can meet twentieth-century standards. It is a faith. Likewise, there is no scientific evidence that such a resurrection never occurred. That, too, is a faith, though less obviously so in an age dominated by science. Dr. Ole Kristoffer Gjotterud, professor of physics at the University of Oslo in Norway, puts it this way:

> If you put a card in a box for each man who died and one in another box for each man who was resurrected, you would have one card in one box and millions and millions in the other. But I would not take the one card out. This is a question of honesty. . . . I have a feeling that many people are asking the questions wrong. They think that the problem is to get the totality of existence inside their own heads, systematized and organized and well understood. The problem is to stay in this total, rich reality and existence with my head which can ask the questions. It is a matter of openness and willingness and ability to stay with the questions.[1]

In our day, no one can claim that he has all the answers, if he wants an intelligent hearing. All we can do is say where our own particular world view has brought us and perhaps give some inkling as to why we have rejected other world views.

Bertrand Russell

When Bertrand Russell was eighty, he published an essay entitled "How to Grow Old," in which he suggested the best way to overcome the fear of death. That way is:

> to make your interests gradually wider and more impersonal, until bit by bit the walls of the ego recede, and your life becomes increasingly merged in the universal life. An individual human

existence should be like a river—small at first, narrowly contained within its banks, and rushing passionately past boulders and over waterfalls. Gradually the river grows wider, the banks recede, the waters flow more quietly, and in the end, without any visible break, they become merged in the sea, and painlessly lose their individual being.[2]

Russell believed that the old man who can look at life in this way will find contentment in his weariness, for he knows that the things he cares about will be taken up by other hands; he has done what he could.

There is much in this conception of death to commend it to Christians. Egotism is a common, chronic ailment, and to see it eventually receding is encouraging. Openness to life, peace, detachment, reconciliation—all are desirable qualities. We recall that Russell, a highly socialized humanist, paid tribute to what he termed "Christian love." But elements important to those who follow Christ are absent. Personal identity, quite different from egotism, is lost, so what has human life amounted to as it washes into a shoreless sea? Russell's view of death makes human existence possibly seem more precious to the philosopher or to an elitist. But in young persons today without their resources it may evoke the attitude, "If drugs ease the tension or boredom, why not? Nothing has meaning anyhow. Why bother to save a life that is doomed from the start?" Seeds planted in one generation mature in the next and permeate with their odor the intellectual air incoming minds must breathe.

Russell indirectly had learned from the church that it is important to love and serve one's neighbor, but he had rejected the seed from which this conviction sprang—that man is called, valued, and loved by God. Always in the background of his thinking lay the haunting belief that some kind of validity existed behind the work he did, even though God was only a ghost. In his essay "Reflections on My Eightieth Birthday," after speaking of the ambiguities of life, he added, "I was not wrong in thinking that there is such a thing [as truth], and that it deserves our allegiance."[3] He had not surrended the belief that a world of free and happy human beings is possible and worth working for; only the road would be longer than he had thought.

The next generation, however, surveying human nature and affairs without his background, does not always find his surmise convincing. What validates it? Humanism does not have the long-term power of implicit, though subconscious, validation that centuries of faith in God provided. David R. Bell says, "There is something heroic, even desperate, in his [Russell's] ability to stare the facts of human evil in the face and yet still entertain hopes of a more tolerant and free world."[4] Did he subconsciously retain some shred of faith in his ghostly God?

In Bertrand Russell's opinion, there was no personal life after death, although he conceded this could not be proved.[5] He reasoned that the mental continuity of a person lies in his habits and memory. These have been an integral part of the brain, the body, so that when these perish, the person perishes too.

My reading of the New Testament and experience of the Presence lead me to a different conception. I do not see our ongoing personal identity as permanently sustained by our bodies although, manifestly, we need these bodies to operate as human beings in this world. When we begin to respond to the divine word, however it comes, a process of new creation begins within us. That word, coming alive for us and making us alive in a new and awesome sense, does not have to be stored in memory (although it may be) but is intrinsic to what we are at any given moment. As for habit, the divine Presence, if attended to, does not allow us to find comfortable ruts in which to vegetate, but keeps stirring us up to follow the light that is never given as a personal possession, but that continually invites and incites us forward. Even as new persons, we would like the kind of security that the whole animal world is always after, but God does not give it. Rather, he weans us from the need of it. His love for us—not our fluctuating love for him—becomes our security and somewhere, deep within that divine love, our identity is carried.

Does this sound too mystical? It is really quite solid. Dietrich Bonhoeffer, living in prison in the jittery shadow of death, tried to find out who he was, to establish his own identity. In a poem

"Who Am I?"[6] he puts questions to himself: Is he the man others see? the man he appears to himself to be? the same person every day? two persons at the same time? The questions mock him, and he finally concludes, "Whoever I am, Thou knowest, O God, I am thine!" The nearest he could come to finding out who he was lay in the discovery of *whose* he was. His identity was God's secret.

Revelation 2:17 once opened up a similar insight for me. It is a seed thought, hidden in a mysterious symbol: "I will give him [the one who overcomes] a white stone, with a new name written on the stone which no one knows except him who receives it." Does this suggest that the revelation of what each person is lies in the future with God? A number of years later, I discovered that Lynn Harold Hough had found the same meaning in this passage that occurred to me. He wrote, "The new name represents the individual personality achieved only through the grace of Christ. He is a new man; but he is not a new man just like every other new man. He is eternally something individual, and different, and eternally prized by God."[7] Again Dr. Hough says, "There is much which he possesses in common with others; but what is done for him is done for him alone. The subtle integrity of the individual life is forever safe with Christ."[8] In his letter to the Colossians, Paul says, "You have died, and your life is hid with Christ in God (Col. 3:3)." Death here refers not to physical death, but to a radical conversion (fast or slow) that puts God, instead of selfish desires, at the center of one's existence. Could we not say, "Your identity is hid with Christ in God"? Is that not what Paul meant centuries before the psychological concept of identity emerged?

Returning to Bertrand Russell's image of rivers flowing on to be lost in the sea, there is a peace that may appeal to a Christian, especially if he has had a stormy life, involving difficult relations with other persons, but there is no reason why peace cannot inhere in human relations when God is loved. The survival of individuality does not carry forward our sharply etched American individualism with its strong connotation of separation and competition. No longer islands of thought, feeling, purpose, lonely and isolated from others, we shall be fully united in Christ.

Some practical minds may be impatient with such visions and fire a volley of difficulties at what they regard as wishful thinking: What of those who die in infancy and childhood? What of those who never heard of Jesus? What of those who listened to his teachings but rejected them? I do not pretend to have the answers to these questions, but I shall not allow my inability to solve such problems to push me toward rejection of the meaning I have found in experience with the living Christ. It is just as puzzling to account for the presence of meaning if the world is assumed to be meaningless, as it is to account for the presence of meaninglessness if the world is assumed to have meaning. There is no reason why the burden of the affirmative should be placed upon religion; it all depends on how one states the premise.

Simone de Beauvoir

The closing pages of Simone de Beauvoir's *Force of Circumstance* are poignant with the pain of passing years that have been fulfilling, and yet have left her unfulfilled, "gypped." But in her recent book *The Coming of Age* she says, "This sweeping away of fetishes and illusions is the truest, most worth-while of all the contributions brought by age. . . . I should never have dreamt of that absolute whose absence I lamented at the end of *La Force des choses*."[9] She quotes the words of Yeats, "Life is a long preparation for something that never happens."[10] There comes a time when a man discovers that he is going nowhere except to the grave. The calm realism (from the atheistic viewpoint) of this last book, to one who has loved Simone de Beauvoir through her writings, is more distressing than the rebelliousness of her earlier works.

She had given thought to the Christian beliefs expressed by her fellow countrymen. Victor Hugo, for example, had looked forward to his death with an easy mind. He had said, "I believe in God; I believe in the soul. I am old; I am going to die. I shall see God. See God! Talk to him! What a tremendous event! What shall I say to him? I often think about it. I am getting ready."[11] To her, this fancied God was "another Hugo." There is surely a point to her question: would it not have been more appropriate to wonder what God would say to him? She notes that he died without agreeing to see a priest.

Her mother, too, had refused priestly help at the last. This was embarrassing to Simone, for she felt her mother's friends would think she had imposed her atheism between her mother and the church when it was within her power to do so. As a matter of fact, she had inquired repeatedly about her mother's wish to see a priest, only to have it brushed aside with the comment, "God is kind." The Benedictine monk who was my friend once told me that it was the task of a priest to make himself unnecessary. Victor Hugo and Mme. de Beauvoir were not rejecting the church, but they had reached their destination. The sacramental bridges were behind them.

Although both were Christians, Hugo had anticipated death while Mme. de Beauvoir had fought it, through hideous suffering, to her last breath. How can one account for this? I asked the nurses: Can religious persons meet death better (with less fear and resistance) than irreligious persons? Most of the nurses with whom I talked were of the opinion that Christian faith enabled patients to meet death more calmly, but one nurse said she thought faith had less to do with this than temperament and ethnic background. If the latter should chance to be right, could this be due to the fact that Christians have not yet been able to get their faith together so as to perceive clearly how its time sense and its whole apprehension of reality differ from that of conflicting ideologies?

Speaking for herself, Simone de Beauvoir says, "Old age changes our relationship with time." As a young person, she had never thought of an end to her time; her future seemed infinite. Even at the age of forty-five, it stretched away interminably. At sixty-five, a boundary mark appeared, hard, limiting, Jean-Paul Sartre called it a wall. The future, once so full of meaning and promise, is now diminishing; the past has frozen. The moments, once bearing her forward into exciting new projects, will soon fall into ashes and the grave will swallow them up.[12]

If Christians were honest, would they have to say that this is their experience too? We have already given two conflicting answers to that question. But let us look deeper. What is responsible for this cleavage? Does Christian faith have a different sense of reality that, if fully grasped, sees a door where many see a wall? The tragedy of divisions among Christians is that we have not yet been able to get our faith together so that it can be seen outside our own ranks for what it is. No outside pressures can cement that faith; it must cohere from within our experience of the living Christ. Let me illustrate this from two deep cleavages that need healing.

1. There is the division between liberals and conservatives. Fundamentalists, using the term loosely, are constantly accused of being otherworldly; sometimes the criticism is justified. In my adolescence, our little church used to sing a chorus, "This world is not my home." It was never intended as a summons away from the people of this earth, but rather from preoccupation with goals limited to this life. We felt we were not building permanent homes here—an obvious but usually overlooked fact. We were pilgrims, moving toward a fatherland where our long-term residence and citizenship lay. While not consciously indifferent to social issues, they seemed temporary and were not our central concern.

Liberals, on the other hand, are accused of being this-worldly. No one knows the meaning of death and what will follow it, they may imply, but we do know the love and justice God requires his people to work for here on earth. Without in the least wishing to deny transtemporal realities, they may appear to overlook them in intense commitment to social projects here on earth.

If the time orientation of liberals and conservatives could be combined, every Christian would have a chance to see that the new culture into which he has been born, through his response to the divine word, is fully concerned with this earth, where we make our present homes and where each of us must carve out his personal mission with God, but that it is just as fully committed to a deepening relationship with our Lord and movement toward the world beyond. Moreover, the world itself would see that the

Christian life is something else, that it has a wholly new perspective on time.

2. Then there is the division between Catholics and Protestants. For many years, Catholic churches stressed the suffering and death of Jesus on behalf of mankind.[13] Young persons, sensitive to this teaching, were drawn into religious orders where the ideal of self-renunciation and suffering with Christ was kept before them. A young Catholic friend of mine, an artist, told me a decade or so ago that she had never heard the Easter message consciously until she was an adult; the crucifixion was the scene.

Protestant churches, on the other hand, have gloried in the empty cross. One can attend a three-hour Good Friday service, frequently held under ecumenical auspices, and see almost empty churches. Worshipers come and go, staying as long as they can or are inclined to remain. But every church will be filled to capacity on Easter, with Palm Sunday a close second in attendance. Only a handful will have exposed themselves at any depth to the memory of Jesus' sorrow and pain.

This failure on the part of our divided churches to celebrate the depths and heights together and with united attention leaves the world with an image of self-denial on the one hand and, on the other, ephemeral optimism. Assuredly, society's time and life sense is not jarred to any great extent by the Christian witness in such divided terms.

The impact of a clearly conjoined this-worldly/otherworldly, crucifixion-resurrection orientation would help to free the individual Christian of fear of his approaching death-crisis and alert the world to the witness that Christians intend to devote themselves unreservedly to the interests of God's kingdom as long as they stay on earth and that they expect to go on living fully when they leave.

The difference between the attitudes of Victor Hugo and Mme. de Beauvoir toward dying may have stemmed from the fact that the former had the intellectual resources for a broad, deep understanding of his faith, whereas the latter saw only the folk emphasis upon suffering without a clear grasp of the implications of Jesus' triumph for her. Victor Hugo had internalized the Christian world view while Mme. de Beauvoir, even though she felt the kindness of God in the midst of her agony, had only the crucifix to look at; the empty cross was not there.

Eugenia Price

Her conversion as a bright, young atheist with an established career in communications brought Eugenia Price many invitations to speak before churches, stressing the conversion experience, but she was wise enough not to allow herself to be stampeded into an activism that would have precluded opportunity for prayer and thoughtful weighing of her future work. Her speaking and writing brought pleas for help in solving personal problems and inquiries into her views as a Christian. Why do some persons die so young while others live too long? What meaning can the critically handicapped find in life? How does one deal with grief, failure, and anguish in unrelieved suffering? "Sick of glib responses" herself, Eugenia Price says in her recent book *No Pat Answers* that we need a person-to-person being together where we can "weep, cry out, struggle—even rebel—*with Christ*."[14] Her dealing with what has been called traditionally "the problem of evil" is not academic. It is open to continuing experience with God, but does not preach or tell people how they ought to feel in any given circumstance.

A sophisticated person may criticize her approach as simplistic. Without doubt, if one is searching for erudite analysis and methodical steps toward the resolution of the problem of human suffering, he will not find it here. But is that what most people want from religion? Is it what the sophisticated individual himself wants in the moment of grave personal crisis? Man being what he is will always wrestle theologically with the ultimate questions, but it is hardly simplistic to treat them in other terms, as though any answers we cannot humanly devise boil down to begging the question.

A simplistic handling of issues occurs when a very complex subject is oversimplified. In this last century, the physical universe we inhabit appears to be far more complicated than anything man, a few generations ago, could have conceived by the most elastic imagination. Therefore, it was believed systematic thought about God must take this new knowledge into account if it is to be worthy of the respectful consideration of educated persons. There seems no middle ground: either we take what has been called biblical revelation and build a transcendent system that stands over against the knowledge of this world, challenging it, or we build systems that attempt to correlate religious knowledge with other kinds of knowledge. We choose, for example, beween Barth and those in his wide orbit, or we lean toward Tillich and the many modifications of his thought. New theologies sprout in all directions, tending toward emphasis upon the transcendence of God or upon process.

But if we believe that Jesus has anything to do with these ruminations, it should be clear that he did not spend his life in the temple with the theologians of his day, much as such a career in the steps of Samuel may have appealed to him at the age of twelve. It was the common people who heard him gladly when he spoke in concrete, earthy, parabolic terms. The parables, to be sure, are far from simple, but they do offer field glasses that any person can adjust so as to bring a blurred issue into focus at his own level of insight. Perhaps it is not the problems themselves that are so complex as the polluted, murky atmosphere through which we try to observe them. If the sale of her books is an indication, Eugenia Price is able to meet many lay persons where they live and help them to see better.

Academic questions regarding life and death are not likely to be answerable, with scientific assurance, in the foreseeable future. That leaves us between agnosticism or atheism, on the one side, and the simplistic stance (from the intellectual point of view) of confidence in God on the other.

If we pose the problem of death in a theological way, it is customary to ask whether man is immortal or whether he does, in fact, reach the end of his existence as a person in death. A minority of theologians today will opt, with the Greeks, for immortality. Those with strong faith believe in resurrection; others fumble for an answer that will make it possible for them to feel fulfilled by death itself, to be reconciled to their mortality. I believe that one can argue for the immortality of the *new creation in Christ,* or for resurrection, on the basis of the New Testament documents themselves but this, to my mind, poses the problem of the future life in the wrong way.

There are two simple facets to New Testament thought that may be overlooked in the search to satisfy human curiosity as to what lies beyond the grave. These answers are given in Christian experience as part of its very substance. Let us look at them.

1. Life is the gift of God, both this life and the one to come. Even in our day, one point is clear: no one has willed himself into existence. His origin is extra-human. If there is an immortality of the human spirit, then, judging from any evidence we have at hand, it is a bestowed immortality, nothing we can fashion for ourselves. Life, whether immortal or resurrected, is the gift of God. The New Testament records are filled with this consciousness.

2. Further, the good news the New Testament proclaims is neither that we are immortal nor that we shall live again, but rather that we are loved by God. We are not orphans, tossed out accidentally as some strange mutation in a blind process. Someone knows we are here and has an eye on us, individually and collectively, although this someone, as far as we can see, does remarkably little interfering with our decisions and programs. The good news is that, loved by God, loved into life, both physical and spiritual, by him, we shall be "forever with the Lord." It makes little difference, then, whether consciousness goes on without interruption following death, or whether we "sleep," unconscious until awakened. In either event, we are with him. God's presence with us, to which the Bible and the church bear witness, is confirmed in the experience of those who take seriously the call to love him with the whole heart, soul, mind, and strength, and to love their neighbors as themselves.

Hope for a future life will not be held with any assurance by those who want God only to alleviate their fear of death. Such hope can be held confidently only by those who start with God and open themselves to his love. To try to tack Christian hope onto a life that measures its good in material terms is impossible.

The "Easter message" eludes those who do not sincerely seek God and who do not care about their neighbors. It sounds more hollow year after year to them until, finally, they decide there is nothing to it and abandon pretense. This is not surprising. What we are able to believe about triumph over death is inherent in what God has been to us in life. From any other point of view, hope of survival *is* simplistic, though this has nothing to do with whether or not we do in fact live after death.

The Apostle Paul

I have mentioned that I came under the influence of Paul's thought while still in high school. Since then, I have studied many brands of philosophy, but have found nothing that offered more stability and promise (not to mention credibility) for the human spirit and community. Historically and today, we all have our presuppositions and focus of attention. No one in this late twentieth century is in any better position to offer final truth than Paul was. Whatever we may select as the standard by which our lives are to be guided, faith in something is at the root. The alternatives are not religious faith or scientific knowledge. Science has no knowledge of the ultimate. Paul's faith, so far-reaching, so adaptable to any fresh manifestation of God, so sure of God among the many systems of man, seemed to call me into an experience rather than toward the adoption of a set pattern of belief. Speaking to my whole person rather than to my mind alone, he moved me toward an experience that found revelation bubbling up in life rather than limited to a system of ideas superimposed by persons living two thousand years ago.

But two further observations must be made: 1. My experience verified Paul's witness, despite the intervening centuries. When Christ is Lord, he does lead into the epiphanies that make life whole and exciting. 2. The Christian world view is not based on fantasy, but rooted in history. Is there not as much danger of reducing history to fantasy as there is of blowing fantasy up into history? The Bible can speak for itself. There is no need to update it in the light of any century that will itself soon be only a memory. If the central biblical message is proclaimed, sociological irrelevancies will drop away. It is necessary only *to get the message through* to the next generation, not to take it apart and then try to reassemble it.

Paul spoke frequently about death and the future life, but I shall mention only three points, possibly not the most important ones, but the most formative in my case. The first is found in 1 Corinthians 2. Paul is wrestling there with the difference between human and divine wisdom. He is contemplating a prayer of Isaiah[15] who believed God to be the Father who guides with integrity those who keep his ways in mind. Then, Paul quotes what impressed him most:

> What no man ever saw or heard,
> What no man ever thought could happen,
> Is the very thing God prepared for those who love him.
> —1 Corinthians 2:9, TEV[16]

This recalls John's record of Jesus' saying, "I go to prepare a place for you (John 14:2)." All through my religious development, I have been aware of a God who goes ahead, who is in every situation before we get there, who is always coming to meet us, who is never taken by surprise but who constantly surprises us. This might be called providence which means, literally, seeing ahead. One can pray to a God like this with confidence that he will shed light on the way. His awareness of us, the assistance we can receive from him in doing right and facing death are beyond anything that we can imagine independently of the historic witness to it.

A second teaching of Paul that took root in my mind very early is found in the fifth chapter of 2 Corinthians. He has already been talking about the future life in the fourth chapter and now says, "We know that when this tent we live in—our body here on earth—is torn down, God will have a house in heaven for us to live in, a home he himself made, which will last for ever."

To twentieth-century man, this sounds fantastic. Where is heaven located? Does this new house mean reincarnation? Since man is the highest form of being visible on earth, it is extremely hard for him to accept the idea that there may be means to knowledge and forms of existence inaccessible to his understanding in this life, but perhaps we should try to entertain such a possibility.

From a scientific point of view, we are limited to what can come through our senses. As we saw in the discussion of paranormal experience, however, there are those who think that our senses can be extended far beyond what they are now able to perceive, and a few persons suggest that we may have senses that we have not yet discovered. Is it so hard to conceive of realities somewhere that are beyond the reach of human sensibility in this life?

A facet of my own experience may help to make this possibility clearer. As a totally color-blind person, color is nonexistent for me. I can see objects people tell me are red, for example, but I have never seen red. I must take the word of those who have the equipment to perceive it that it is there. Try as I will to understand, others are not able to make colors real to me. "Is green beautiful?" I ask, and when friends say yes, I try to find out more: "But envy is not a beautiful quality, so why do people say 'green with envy'?" The same thing is true of yellow. On the one hand, people talk about the glorious golden sunshine and, on the other, they call cowards "yellow." It is frustrating and beyond my comprehension to follow conversations that involve color. Is it not quite possible that there are other forms of experience that are missed at this stage of existence because we lack the equipment for receiving them? I do not find Paul's thought here, on the mystery of death, as difficult to comprehend as the mystery of color. People raise the question as to whether or not intelligent life exists on other planets. Would we make our earthly concept of intelligence the norm for all the universes?

Farther along in life, Paul expresses his faith in other terms. Much suffering is behind him. He has not lived in an ivory tower, but has been on the frontier with Christ, frequently facing hostility for the good news he proclaimed, often persecuted for his proclamation. A prisoner, he does not know what lies ahead of him and weighs the alternatives of life and death in his letter to the Philippians, summing them up in the words, "For me to live is Christ, and to die is gain (Phil. 1:21)." There is no boundary line here, no wall—one might almost say no exit, for his highway of life carries him toward death as a bridge to the future. He lives toward it, making the most of each day, not looking back with nostalgia for the past.

The Presence

When, in terror and anguish, I saw my mother in her casket, the fear of death was removed cleanly and permanently in the knowledge that she would not be buried; she had gone. In later years, it became clear to me that this had been a silent meeting with God. Who else could have acted so decisively and lastingly in such a crisis?

The Presence has said very little to me about death over the years, but a few incidents stand out. Once I lay watching an insect that was soon going to end its existence buzzing about a hot light bulb and, feeling a momentary identification with it, I said to Christ, "That is how your light affects me, and even if I knew that I would be burned to death, I would want to respond all the same." In what seemed to be patient pain, the Presence answered, "This light is for life, not death."

On another occasion, drawn into meditation on Jesus' word from the cross, "My God, my God, why hast thou forsaken me?" I saw what negates description and heard, "I went out alone that you might never have to know what it is to go alone."

Then, some months ago, I had what seemed to be my second significant dream. As I was climbing the hill to our home, tiredness overwhelmed me, and I thought, "I don't believe I can make it." All at once, I became aware of a strange, soft breeze all about me, and the Presence spoke gently with a touch of humor, "Lean back in it. It will hold you—like a chair." Complying in the same light vein, I noticed we were moving, the houses were passing on either side, and I thought, "It *is* going to carry me clear to the top of the hill." Glancing to the right again, I saw an unfamiliar landscape and, in the same split second, wakened to the realization that I had been dreaming about death.

NOTES

Introduction

1. Dr. Abraham A. Low worked with this principle in mind. The story of his life and work is told by Neil and Margaret Rau, *My Dear Ones* (Englewood Cliffs, N.J.: Prentice-Hall, 1971). Recovery groups are an outgrowth of his labor and his own books are well worth study.

Chapter 1. Experience: God and Death

1. John Habgood, *Truths in Tension; Perspectives in Religion and Science* (New York: Holt, Rinehart and Winston, 1965), p. 129.

2. F. M. Esfandiary, *Optimism One, the Emerging Radicalism* (New York: W. W. Norton, 1970), quoted by Wes Thomas and Jeremy Wiesen, "The Case for Optimism," *The Futurist* VI, Apr. 1972, p. 68.

3. Nigel Calder, *The Mind of Man* (New York: Viking Press, 1971), pp. 29-30. Calder is a former editor of *The New Scientist,* and at the time of this book's appearance was science correspondent for *The New Statesman.*

4. For his musing on this point, see *The Autobiography of Bertrand Russell 1872-1914* (Boston: Little, Brown & Co., 1951), I, 66-67.

5. Theodore Roszak, *The Making of a Counter-Culture* (Garden City, N.Y.: Doubleday, 1968), p. 81.

6. Russell, op. cit., I, 220.

7. Russell, op. cit., *1914-1944,* II, 59.

8. C. A. Joyce, ed., *My Call to Preach* (London: Marshall, Morgan & Scott, 1968), p. 53. The statement is made by the Rev. John Lambert.

9. Ibid., p. 90. This statement is made by the Rev. Derek J. Prime.

10. Russell, op. cit., I, 343.

11. Russell, op. cit., II, 122.

12. Ibid., p. 121.

13. *Autobiography of Bertrand Russell, 1944-1969* (New York: Simon & Schuster, 1969), III, 24-25.

14. Russell, op. cit., II, 231.

15. Simone de Beauvoir, *Memoirs of a Dutiful Daughter,* tr. James Kirkup (Middlesex, England: Penguin Books, 1963), p. 140.

16. Simone de Beauvoir, *Force of Circumstance*, tr. Richard Howard (New York: G. P. Putnam's Sons, 1965), p. 46.

17. de Beauvoir, *Memoirs*, p. 232.

18. de Beauvoir, *Force of Circumstance*, p. 354.

19. Simone de Beauvoir, *The Prime of Life*, tr. Peter Green (Middlesex, England: Penguin Books, 1965), pp. 207-8.

20. Ibid., p. 208. The statement is qualified as applying to those who live under "specially privileged conditions."

21. de Beauvoir, *Memoirs*, p. 138.

22. Ibid.

23. de Beauvoir, *Force of Circumstance*, p. 425.

24. Ibid., p. 451.

25. Simone de Beauvoir, *A Very Easy Death*, tr. Patrick O'Brian (Middlesex, England: Penguin Books, 1969), p. 92.

26. Rudolf Bultmann, *Faith and Understanding*, ed. Robert W. Funk, tr. Louise Pettibone Smith (New York: Harper & Row, 1969), p. 50.

27. See Richard E. Sherrell, "The Case Against God in Contemporary French Drama," *Religion in Life* XXXI, Autumn 1962, pp. 610ff. Also Richard E. Sherrell, *The Human Image: Avant-Garde and Christian* (Richmond, Va.: John Knox Press, 1969).

28. John G. Taylor, *The Shape of Minds to Come* (New York: Weybright & Talley, 1971), p. 262.

29. Eugenia Price, *The Burden Is Light: The Autobiography of a Transformed Pagan* (Westwood, N.J.: Fleming H. Revell, 1956). This is a small book, and I shall not indicate pages.

30. Eugenia Price, *Woman to Woman* (Grand Rapids, Mich.: Zondervan, 1959), p. 240.

31. Ibid., p. 239.

32. Bertrand Russell records the incident in his essay, "Why I Took to Philosophy," *Portraits from Memory and Other Essays* (New York: Simon & Schuster, 1956), pp. 14-15.

33. Jacques Barzun, *Science, the Glorious Entertainment* (New York: Harper & Row, 1964), p. 81.

34. Calder, op. cit., p. 258.

35. Ibid., p. 253.

36. An interesting conversation between Freud and Sachs, revealing Freud's attitude on this matter, is found in Irving Stone's thoroughly researched novel, *The Passions of the Mind* (Garden City, N.Y.: Doubleday, 1971), p. 103.

37. Carl G. Jung, "The Soul and Death," *The Meaning of Death*, ed. Herman Feifel (New York: McGraw-Hill, 1959), p. 12.

38. Computers with IQs over 150 have been forecast. See Paul Dickson, *Think Tanks* (New York: Atheneum, 1971), p. 327; see also Hubert L. Dreyfus' scholarly study, *What Computers Can't Do: A Critique of Artificial Reason* (New York: Harper & Row, 1972).

39. Calder, op. cit., p. 262.

40. In this connection, Frederick E. Trinklein has edited a popularly written book, *The God of Science*, in which scientists express themselves on various questions (Grand Rapids, Mich.: Wm. B. Eerdmans, 1971).

Chapter 2. Experience: Christian, Mystical, and Paranormal

1. Participating churches are: The African Methodist Episcopal, The African Methodist Episcopal Zion, The Christian (Disciples of Christ), The Christian Methodist Episcopal, The Episcopal, The Presbyterian Church in the U.S., The United Church of Christ, The United Methodist, and the United Presbyterian Church in the U.S.A.

2. This is a paraphrase, but see Matthew 22:34-41; Mark 12:28-35; Luke 10:25-29.

3. The question leads to the story of the good Samaritan, found in Luke 10:29-38.

4. These simple definitions are given by Evelyn Underhill, *Practical Mysticism* (New York: E. P. Dutton, 1914), p. 3.

5. See Stephen C. Pepper, *World Hypotheses: A Study in Evidence* (Berkeley: University of California Press, 1962—first published in 1942); note especially p. 119. Pepper does not think mysticism can pass as a world view because it lacks "scope" (see p. 134).

6. Richard E. Haymaker, *From Pampas to Hedgerows and Downs: A Study of W. H. Hudson* (New York: Bookman Associates, 1954), p. 304.

7. Arthur Gibson, *The Faith of the Atheist* (New York: Harper & Row, 1968.) Other writers treated by Gibson are Sartre, Camus, Lenin, Nietzsche, and Alexander.

8. *Autobiography of Bertrand Russell, 1944-1969* (New York: Simon & Schuster, 1969), III, 51.

9. See volume VI of the series "New Directions in Theology Today," Roger L. Shinn, *Man, The New Humanism* (Philadelphia: Westminster Press, 1968), p. 176.

10. Frank Laubach will be remembered as the "apostle of literacy" who wrote both devotional books and mission studies. The spiritual experience that guided him in this instance is recorded in *Letters by a Modern Mystic.*

11. Dom A. Graham, *The End of Religion: Autobiographical Explorations* (New York: Harcourt Brace Jovanovich, 1971), pp. 103-291.

12. See Jack Forem, *Transcendental Meditation: Maharishi Mahesh Yogi and the Science of Creative Intelligence* (New York: E. P. Dutton, 1973). See also John Robbins and David Fisher, *Tranquility Without Pills: All About Transcendental Meditation* (New York: Peter Wyden, 1972). This movement is also known as "The Science of Creative Intelligence." Many magazine articles have been published, especially in scientific and education periodicals.

13. See Ignacio L. Gotz, *The Psychedelic Teacher: Drugs, Mysticism, and Schools* (Philadelphia: Westminster Press, 1972), pp. 43ff. A more cautious statement is made by Edgar Draper, M.D., "An Illusion's Past," in *Healer of the Mind*, ed. Paul E. Johnson (Nashville: Abingdon Press, 1972), p. 108.

14. I have chosen the one incident in Simone de Beauvoir's experience for an illustration but, a precocious child, she was put off on a number of occasions by a stereotyped approach that did not come close to meeting her need. The occasion I describe seems to have been quite crucial, however, and, without doubt, sad instances of failure to meet the needs of children, precocious and otherwise, could be cited from any church or school.

15. For an interesting article dealing with the implications of parapsychology

for religion, see J. Schoneberg Setzer, "Parapsychology: Religion's Basic Science," *Religion in Life* XXXIX, Winter 1970.

16. Daniel Logan, *The Reluctant Prophet: The Autobiography of a Clairvoyant* (Garden City, N.Y.: Doubleday, 1968).

17. Doris Agee, *Edgar Cayce on ESP*, ed. Hugh L. Cayce (New York: Coronet Communications, Paperback Library, 1969), pp. 7-8.

18. For early data regarding Ford, see Sherwood Eddy, *You Will Survive Death* (New York: Rinehart & Co., 1950), p. 109. He has been discussed by many writers. See also Arthur Ford as told to Jerome Ellison, *The Life Beyond Death* (New York: G. P. Putnam's Sons, 1971).

19. David L. Miller, "Orestes: Myth and Drama as Catharsis," *Myths, Dreams, and Religion*, ed. Joseph Campbell (New York: E. P. Dutton, 1970), pp. 30-31.

20. Nicolas Berdyaev, *Dream and Reality* (New York: Macmillan, 1951), p. 183.

21. Harmon H. Bro, *Dreams in the Life of Prayer: The Approach of Edgar Cayce* (New York: Harper & Row, 1970), p. 43.

22. The dream experience of Joseph (Genesis 37ff.) will be recalled. There are many other biblical examples. Mary McDermott Shideler, *Consciousness of Battle* (Grand Rapids, Mich.: Wm. B. Eerdmans, 1960), has a chapter on "The Place of the Dream," in which she describes and discusses a dream of her own. I shall relate such an experience also.

23. This is considered at some length by Ian G. Barbour, *Issues in Science and Religion* (Englewood Cliffs, N.J.: Prentice-Hall, 1966). A shorter and very useful book is his *Science and Secularity* (New York: Harper & Row, 1970). H. Richard Neff in chapter 2 of his *Psychic Phenomena and Religion: ESP, Prayer, Healing, Survival* (Philadelphia: Westminster Press, 1971), considers and evaluates the work done by Dr. Rhine and others on ESP.

24. Martin Ebon, *They Knew the Unknown* (New York: World Publishing Co., 1971), p. 151. A leading parapsychologist, Ebon has also written in the field of the psychology of economics and public affairs.

25. Ibid., p. 153.

26. Neff, op. cit., p. 170.

27. Logan, op. cit., p. 171.

Many books on the occult are appearing. John P. Newport, *Demons, Demons, Demons* (Nashville: Broadman Press, 1972), has written a small book that examines the subject in the light of biblical texts. John Godwin, *Occult America* (Garden City, New York: Doubleday, 1972), gives a full and popular account of the subject. David P. Young, *A New World in the Morning: The Biopsychological Revolution* (Philadelphia: Westminster Press, 1972), discusses whether or not a drug-induced experience can be labeled mystical or religious (p. 83). See also Roger C. Palms, *The Christian and the Occult* (Valley Forge, Pa.: Judson Press, 1972).

Chapter 3. The Book That Covers a Voice

1. Colossians may be a post-Pauline letter, but the thought is his.

2. There are new approaches to the Bible today, and several have been helpful to me: Wilfred Cantwell Smith, "The Study of Religion and the Study of the

Bible," *Journal of the American Academy of Religion*, XXXIX, no. 2 (June 1971), pp. 131-40; James William McClendon, "Biography as Theology," *Cross Currents*, XXI, no. 4 (Fall 1971), pp. 415-31; Vernard Eller, "How Jacques Ellul Reads the Bible," *The Christian Century*, LXXXIX, no. 43 (Nov. 29, 1972), pp. 1212-15; Gregory Baum, "The Bible as Norm," *The Ecumenist*, IX, no. 5 (July-Aug. 1971), pp. 71-77; Loyal D. Rue, "Michael Polanyi, and the Critical Approach to Sacred Texts," *Dialog*, XII (Spring 1973), pp. 117-20; Jay G. Williams, "Exegesis—Eisegesis: Is There a Difference?" *Theology Today*, XXX, no. 3 (Oct. 1973).

3. Ira Progoff, "Walking Dream and Living Myth," *Myths, Dreams, and Religion*, ed. Joseph Campbell (New York: E. P. Dutton, 1970), pp. 178-96 (see ch. 2, n. 22).

4. Hugh Thomson Kerr, "The Song of Songs," *The Interpreter's Bible*, Vol. 5 (Nashville: Abingdon Press, 1956), p. 98.

5. Simone de Beauvoir, *Memoirs of a Dutiful Daughter*, tr. James Kirkup (Middlesex, England: Penguin Books, 1963), p. 272, *also* sought *proof* of God's existence.

6. Frances Ridley Havergal is best known for her hymn, "Take My Life and Let It Be." I have quoted the lines of her poem "Enough for Me" from memory. See *Sourcebook of Poetry*, ed. Thomas A. Bryant (Grand Rapids, Mich.: Zondervan, 1968).

7. Piri Thomas, *Down These Mean Streets* (New York: New American Library, 1971), p. 301. Where this prayer has taken Piri may be learned from his book *Savior, Savior, Hold My Hand* (Garden City, N.Y.: Doubleday, 1972).

8. Dr. Purdy wrote the Introduction and Exegesis on "The Epistle to the Hebrews" for *The Interpreter's Bible*, Vol. 11, as well as other books and articles.

9. Josephine Sanger Lau, *Beggar Boy of Galilee* (New York: Abingdon-Cokesbury Press, 1946).

10. An example of this appears in Numbers 31:15-19. Articles on war in Bible times appear in *The Interpreter's Dictionary of the Bible*, Vol. R-Z (Nashville: Abingdon Press, 1962), pp. 796-805.

11. Arthur A. Cohen, *The Myth of the Judaeo-Christian Tradition and Other Dissenting Essays* (New York: Harper & Row, 1970), pp. xiv-xv.

12. The book was published in paperback by The Westminster Press, 1970. A remedy for the situation was not developed.

13. Cf. Gijs Bouwman, S.V.D., "Can We Base Our Spiritual Life Today on the Bible?" *Secularization and Spirituality, Concilium*, Vol. 49, tr. Theodore L. Westow (New York: Paulist Press, 1969). Also Richard Kroner, *Between Faith and Thought: Reflections and Suggestions* (New York: Oxford University Press, 1966), pp. 96-97.

14. Abraham Joshua Heschel, *God in Search of Man: A Philosophy of Judaism* (New York: Farrar, Straus & Co., 1955), p. 260.

15. Ibid., p. 259.

16. Amos N. Wilder, *The New Voice: Religion, Literature, Hermeneutics* (New York: Herder & Herder, 1969), p. 71.

17. James Tunstead Burtchaell, C.S.C., *Catholic Theories of Biblical Inspira-*

tion Since 1810: A Review and Critique (New York: Cambridge University Press, 1969), pp. 304-5.

18. Eugenia Price, *Discoveries Made from Living My New Life* (Grand Rapids, Mich.: Zondervan, 1970 ed.), p. 66.

19. Cohen, op. cit., pp. 29-30.

20. Cf. Brevard S. Childs, *Biblical Theology in Crisis* (Philadelphia: Westminster Pess, 1970), pp. 99-100.

21. See context: Exodus 21:22-25.

22. Matthew 5. Note especially verses 38ff.

Chapter 4. That One Talent

1. For a fascinating, pictorial account of a young couple who have been serving as copastors, see Barbara Gerlach Mack and John Mack, "Equal in Marriage Equal in Ministry," *A.D.*, United Church Herald Edition, I, no. 3 (Nov. 1972).

2. I have told Mrs. Ives' story in chapter 5 of my book *When the Minister Is a Woman* (New York: Holt, Rinehart & Winston, 1970).

3. Harold Greenwald has written a social and psychological study on *The Elegant Prostitute* (New York: Ballantine Books, 1958). The ca˙ studies deal with girls who are not in prison, and seem to me to support a ˙ew I have long held: that women in this work have had tragic childhoods or early traumatic experiences. A novel like Nelson Algren's *Never Come Morning* illustrates my point. I heard Mr. Algren describe the incident that led to the writing of this book, and felt his motivation was religious, though he might not agree. Should not Christian people learn to distinguish between books that make the ghetto scene poignantly real, because the authors grew up there (even though they use foul language), and books that are pornographic? There is a vast difference.

Chapter 5. The People of God—Where?

1. A modern book that makes the same point is Helmut Thielicke's *How To Believe Again* (Philadelphia: Fortress Press, 1972).

2. The author is English. I regret that I cannot remember when and where his book was published.

3. Many years later, I discovered a small booklet in the "Paternoster Series" that throws light on what happened: Père de la Taille, S.J., *Contemplative Prayer* (London: Burns Oates & Washbourne, 1926); note especially pp. 26-27.

4. Yngve Brilioth, *Eucharistic Faith and Practice: Evangelical and Catholic* (London: Society for Promoting Christian Knowledge, 1930).

5. Holy Communion is celebrated more frequently today (once a month), though this may vary among churches of the denomination.

6. The merger of Congregational Christian and Evangelical and Reformed Churches was imminent, and this pastor feared growing ecumenical trends.

7. The articles are: "What Are You Saying to Protestants?" *Ave Maria*, XCVI, no. 3 (July 21, 1962), pp. 20-21 and "St. Thomas Confronts a Protestant," *Cross and Crown: A Thomistic Quarterly of Spiritual Theology*, XIV, no. 4 (Dec. 1962), pp. 432-44.

8. The phrase is used without theological precision.

9. Among Protestants, theological consensus is growing; structure is the problem area. But the official Roman Catholic position makes the papacy, for example, a matter of faith.

Chapter 6. Coping with Death

1. A. Herbert Schwartz, M.D., and Jane S. Sturges, "Medical Experimentation on Children," *Should Doctors Play God?* ed. Claude A. Frazier (Nashville: Broadman Press, 1971), p. 88.

2. Cf. John G. Taylor, *The Shape of Minds to Come* (New York: Weybright & Talley, 1971), p. 262 (ch. 1, n. 28).

3. See Cornish Rogers, "Biomedics, Psychosurgery and Laissez-Faire," *The Christian Century*, XC, no. 39 (Oct. 31, 1973).

4. Alice Bergman, R.N., "Is There Not Also a Spirit?" *RN*, May 1972, pp. 46ff.

5. Ibid., p. 80. The page is not noted by the author, who was reading an edition put out by Random House, but will be found in *Notebooks 1935-1942* by Albert Camus (New York: Alfred A. Knopf, 1965), p. 75.

6. Elisabeth Kubler-Ross, *On Death and Dying* (New York: Macmillan, 1970). Her summary of the stages through which the terminally ill patient passes have been quoted frequently: denial and isolation, anger, bargaining, depression, and acceptance. The American Cancer Society has distributed a reprint of Dr. Kubler-Ross's article, "What Is It Like to Be Dying?" published in *American Journal of Nursing*, LXXI, no. 1 (Jan. 1971).

7. See "Keeping Patients Alive: Who Decides? Growing Debate over Medical Ethics," *U.S. News & World Report*, May 22, 1972, p. 45.

8. Ibid. The article notes that in 1957 Pope Pius XII, in an address entitled "The Prolongation of Life," declared "extraordinary measures" such as assistance to the heart and lungs need not be taken to maintain life when irreparable and overwhelming brain damage has occurred.

9. This decision, along with other important data, is specified in an article by Lawrence Mosher, "Where There Is No Hope . . . Why Prolong Life?" reprinted from *The National Observer*, 11501 Columbia Pike, Silver Spring, Md. 20910, March 4, 1972. Pros and cons of the "Death with Dignity" issue are discussed in the *NRTA* (National Retired Teachers Association) *News Bulletin*, XIII, no. 8 (Sept. 1972).

10. The address is 250 West 57 St., New York, N.Y. 10019.

11. Henry A. Davidson, M.D., "'Death by Choice'; The Good and Evil of Euthanasia," *Should Doctors Play God?* op. cit., p. 81.

12. Walter C. Alvarez, M.D., Foreword to Carl G. Carlozzi, *Death and Contemporary Man: The Crisis of Terminal Illness* (Grand Rapids, Mich.: Wm. B. Eerdmans, 1968), pp. 8-9.

13. Eustace Chesser, *Living with Suicide* (London: Hutchinson, 1967); see especially p. 111.

14. See n. 4 of this chapter.

15. Kubler-Ross, op. cit., pp. 19ff.

16. K. R. Eissler, M.D., *The Psychiatrist and the Dying Patient* (New York: International Universities Press, 1955), p. 119.

17. Kurt W. Back, *Beyond Words: The Story of Sensitivity Training and the*

Encounter Movement (New York: Russell Sage Foundation, 1972), p. 18. His discussion of the point is interesting.

18. This is how Cooper opens his review of *The Making of a Psychiatrist* by David S. Wiscott, M.D., in the Nov. 13, 1972 issue, pp. 106ff.

19. Eissler, op. cit., pp. 143ff.

20. Ibid., p. 28. Eissler does not see this as opposed to Freud's later concept of the "death wish." In agreement is Lloyd C. Elam, "A Psychiatric Perspective on Death," *Perspectives on Death*, ed. Liston O. Mills (Nashville: Abingdon Press, 1969), p. 198. Freud's *Thoughts for the Times* is the work under discussion. The point is controversial.

21. Eissler, op. cit., p. 54.

22. See *Healer of the Mind*, ed. Paul E. Johnson (Nashville: Abingdon Press, 1972), ch. 2, n. 16.

23. They have apparently come to this field more recently. Barney G. Glaser and Anselm L. Strauss have done important work in this field. Under the auspices of a six-year research program, financed by the National Institute of Health, they have made several studies: *Time for Dying* (1965), *The Discovery of Grounded Theory* (1967), and *Awareness of Dying* (1968), published by Aldine in Chicago. A part of the same research program is Jeanne Quint's *The Nurse and the Dying Patient* (New York: Macmillan, 1967). A more recent volume dealing extensively with sociological problems regarding death is *The Dying Patient*, ed. Orville G. Brim, Jr., Howard E. Freeman, Sol Levine, Norman A. Scotch, and Greer Williams (New York: Russell Sage Foundation, 1970). It has an excellent bibliography. Peter and Brigitte Berger have introduced a biographical approach to sociology that makes the special needs of old age, illness, and death more visible; *Sociology* (New York: Basic Books, 1972), an introductory textbook with delightful artwork, will appeal to the general reader as well as to the student.

24. Kubler-Ross, op. cit., p. 226.

25. Carlozzi, op. cit., this ch., n. 12, p. 58.

26. Ibid., p. 61. Carlozzi heard the story from Chaplain R. E. Buxbaum.

27. St. Christopher's Hospice, *Annual Report*, 1971-72, p. 4.

28. I am grateful to Dr. Cicely Saunders, who sent me various papers in response to an inquiry.

29. I am grateful to Mrs. Peggy Moss for sending mimeographed materials on Hospice, Inc.

Chapter 7. Exit to Death—or Life?

1. Frederick E. Trinklein, *The God of Science* (Grand Rapids, Mich.: Wm. B. Eerdmans, 1971), pp. 102, 184 (ch. 1, n. 40). Used by permission.

2. Bertrand Russell, *Portraits from Memory and Other Essays* (New York: Simon & Schuster, 1956), pp. 52-53 (ch. 1, n. 37).

3. Ibid., p. 58.

4. David R. Bell, *Bertrand Russell*, "Makers of Modern Thought Series" (Valley Forge, Pa.: Judson Press, 1972), p. 62.

5. Bertrand Russell, *Why I Am Not a Christian* (New York: Simon & Schuster, 1957), p. 89.

6. Dietrich Bonhoeffer, *Letters and Papers from Prison* (England: S.C.M., 1958), p. 173.

7. Lynn Harold Hough, "Exposition: The Revelation of St. John the Divine," *The Interpreter's Bible* (Nashville: Abingdon Press), XII, 387.

8. Ibid., p. 557.

9. Simone de Beauvoir, *The Coming of Age,* tr. Patrick O'Brian (New York: G. P. Putnam's Sons, 1972), p. 492.

10. Ibid., p. 491.

11. Ibid., p. 511. His grandson said, "He saw his end coming, and he spoke to us about it with such untroubled serenity that he never gave us the appalling vision of death."

12. Ibid., see pp. 361ff., 450ff.

13. The emphasis I am noting here is recognized by Roman Catholic theologians and is being corrected. F. X. Durrwell, C.Ss.R., in his book *The Resurrection: A Biblical Study,* tr. Rosemary Sheed (New York: Sheed & Ward, 1960) says, "Not so long ago theologians used to study the Redemption without mentioning the Resurrection at all. . . . In short, Christ's resurrection was shorn of the tremendous significance seen in it by the first Christian teachers, and relegated to the background of the redemptive scheme. Such blindness naturally impoverished the whole theology of the Atonement (p. xxiii)." In the Introduction, Charles Davis, S.T.L., says, "The plain truth is that the average theology of the Redemption is truncated and its intelligibility maimed. The basic reason is the omission of the Resurrection. The resurrection of Christ is essential in the mystery of salvation. To attempt an account of the Redemption without including the Resurrection is to end in an impasse (p. xiii)."

14. Eugenia Price, *No Pat Answers* (Grand Rapids, Mich.: Zondervan, 1972), p. 126.

15. Isaiah 64: note verses 4, 5, and 8.

16. *Good News for Modern Man* (New York: American Bible Society, 1966).

ABOUT THE AUTHOR

Elsie Fuller Gibson is a native of Chicago, a graduate of Taylor University and the Hartford Theological Seminary (B.D., S.T.M.). She is the author of *When the Minister Is a Woman* (Holt, Rinehart & Winston, 1970) and numerous magazine and journal articles.

Mrs. Gibson and her husband, Royal J. Gibson, were both ordained to the ministry of the Congregational Church, Portage, Maine, in 1935. She has been particularly interested in the development of ecumenical ministries, in the search for faith in today's world, and in the role of women in the church's ministry. Mrs. Gibson now resides in Hartford, Connecticut.